Continuing Is the Risk

On Persistence Without Progress

Xiaoqing Wang

This volume provides no directives.

ISBN: 979-8-9947559-2-1

Contents

Chapter 1

Continuing Is the Risk

There is a moment that rarely feels like a moment at all.

Nothing breaks. Nothing collapses. No clear failure appears. What changes is quieter than that. The effort continues, the work remains respectable, and the reasons for staying seem intact. From the outside, it looks indistinguishable from persistence.

From the inside, however, something has already shifted.

This book begins there.

Not at the point of obvious loss, and not at the moment of decisive action, but at the stage where continuing no longer feels optional, yet still feels justified. The project is alive. The relationship is functional. The path forward is visible. And yet, the cost of staying has begun to change in ways that are difficult to name.

Most people do not recognize this stage as dangerous. There is no warning sign for it. Continuing is usually praised, and stopping is usually questioned. Effort is assumed to be additive. Time invested is treated as neutral or even protective.

But continuation is not neutral.

It alters the structure in which future decisions are made. It reshapes what counts as acceptable loss. It quietly changes which exits remain available.

None of this requires failure to begin.

In many cases, the situation improves just enough to justify staying. Small signs of progress appear. Partial rewards arrive. The sense of being "almost there" becomes persistent. These signals do not resolve the uncertainty; they stabilize it.

The risk does not come from choosing wrongly. It comes from allowing continuation itself to redefine the conditions under which choice still exists.

When people describe being "stuck," they often mean something different. They are not immobilized. They are active. They are producing output. They are showing up. The problem is not inactivity, but momentum without directional clarity.

Momentum has weight.

Each additional step increases the cost of reversal, even when no explicit commitment has been made. The longer something continues, the harder it becomes to evaluate it as if it were new. Time does not only accumulate results; it accumulates obligation.

At this stage, effort begins to protect the situation from scrutiny. Stopping would now require explanation. Continuing requires none. The default shifts quietly, without announcement.

This is why many situations become difficult to leave long before they become unbearable to stay in.

The environment rewards continuity while obscuring its effects. Colleagues see consistency. Others see resilience. Past investment is interpreted as evidence of seriousness. These interpretations are not false, but they are incomplete.

What they fail to capture is that continuation changes what future loss will look like.

Loss is rarely sudden at this stage. It stretches. It becomes distributed. Instead of a single decisive cost, it appears as a series of small concessions. Each one feels manageable. None of them feel final.

Together, they form a slope.

On this slope, effort no longer functions as progress. It functions as stabilization. The system adapts around the effort, not toward resolution.

This is not a story of regret. It is not a warning against commitment. It is an examination of how effort, once embedded, begins to shape the space of possible outcomes.

Many people believe they are deciding whether to continue. In reality, continuation has already decided something for them: what they are now willing to tolerate.

The earlier version of themselves might have questioned the situation. The current version maintains it. This difference is not philosophical. It is structural.

As continuation extends, the criteria for evaluation quietly shift. What once would have been unacceptable becomes understandable. What once would have triggered reconsideration becomes noise.

None of this feels dramatic. That is precisely why it works.

By the time the situation is clearly damaging, the cost of exit is no longer comparable to what it once was. The loss did not arrive all at once. It arrived as a gradient.

This book does not ask whether you should continue. It does not suggest that stopping is superior. It does not offer a method for deciding.

It looks instead at what continuation does.

At how effort, sustained beyond a certain point, begins to generate risk not by failing, but by succeeding just enough to remain in motion.

The chapters that follow do not aim to resolve this tension. They describe it.

Because before a decision can be made, the structure in which that decision exists must be visible.

And continuation, once it has begun to reshape that structure, is no longer a neutral act.

This statement can be repeated in slower language. The risk is not waiting somewhere ahead of continuation. The risk is produced by continuation while continuation appears ordinary. The risk is not external to the motion. The risk is carried inside the motion.

To say that continuing is the risk does not mean that continuing is always wrong. It does not convert continuation into error. It does not convert stopping into virtue. It names a structural condition, not a moral verdict. The sentence is diagnostic in tone, not corrective in tone.

The phrase can be restated without changing its center. Continuation is not only a response to risk. Continuation can become the mechanism through which risk is formed. Continuation is not merely exposed to risk. Continuation can actively accumulate risk by sustaining a narrowing frame.

This is not the language of catastrophe. Catastrophe is sudden and visible. This judgment concerns what is gradual and hard to separate from normal effort. The emphasis is on slow transformation, not abrupt collapse. The emphasis is on altered conditions of choice, not dramatic events.

The same thought can be written as a boundary. This is not a claim about courage. This is not a claim about weakness. This is not a claim about discipline. This is not a claim about motivation. The judgment does not interpret personality. It describes what repeated continuation does to the decision environment.

Another boundary can be drawn. This is not a claim that effort has no value. Effort can remain real, serious, and competent. The point is narrower. Effort can remain real while leverage declines.

Effort can remain serious while tolerance shifts. Effort can remain competent while options become harder to access.

The statement can also be heard as a correction of common phrasing. People often speak as if risk belongs to uncertain outcomes only. This chapter places risk inside the process that keeps outcomes in motion. Risk is not only what might happen after deciding. Risk is also what happens while postponing the conditions of deciding.

The meaning does not depend on visible deterioration. Visible deterioration is one possible endpoint. The judgment concerns an earlier interval in which visible stability and structural risk coexist. The coexistence is central. If instability were obvious, the formulation would be unnecessary. It becomes necessary precisely because stability can hide the accumulating cost.

The idea can be repeated through contrast. A threat is often imagined as something that arrives. Here, the threat is something that is maintained. A threat is often imagined as interruption. Here, the threat is uninterrupted motion. A threat is often imagined as deviation. Here, the threat is persistence without re-grounding.

This does not convert continuity into panic. It slows interpretation. It separates the appearance of continuity from the assumption of safety. It refuses the shortcut that says movement equals progress. It refuses the shortcut that says endurance equals protection. It leaves motion visible without granting motion automatic legitimacy.

The sentence can be rewritten in terms of time. The risk is not only in where continuation might end. The risk is in what continuation repeatedly changes before any ending appears. Time is not a neutral container around effort. Time is an active medium that reweights tolerances. Time is the method by which continuation reorganizes what feels normal.

This is not a call to urgency. Urgency would create another compression. Urgency would replace one automatic pattern with another. The judgment does not ask for speed. It asks that continuation stop being treated as inert. It asks that continuation be seen as formative.

The same core can be stated through negation. Continuing is not simply the absence of stopping. Continuing is the presence of repeated reinforcement. Continuing is not empty duration. Continuing is selective repetition. Continuing is not passive extension. Continuing is active conditioning of future interpretation.

Another negation matters. The claim is not that continuation always removes agency. The claim is that continuation can reframe agency before agency is explicitly exercised. Choice can remain technically available while practically narrowed. Choice can remain visible as concept while less reachable as act. This gap between formal possibility and lived accessibility is part of the risk.

The formulation can be recast as a statement about thresholds. Continuation moves thresholds gradually. What once triggered reevaluation can become background noise. What once felt costly can become routine. What once felt temporary can become baseline. Threshold movement is quiet. Quiet movement is easy to mistake for no movement.

This is not a theory of blame. No single decision needs to be mistaken for the structure to appear. No dramatic misjudgment is required. The shape can emerge through reasonable choices repeated under familiar pressure. Reasonable does not mean harmless. Reasonable repetition can still produce a narrowing corridor.

The sentence can be repeated with fewer nouns. Continuing changes what continuing feels like. Continuing changes what stopping costs. Continuing changes what alternatives look like. Continuing changes what questions feel permissible. Continuing changes what future continuation must protect.

This cluster is not rhetorical decoration. It marks that continuation is recursive. Continuation feeds on its own prior continuation. Each cycle supplies justification for the next cycle. Each cycle also supplies additional weight that must be carried. The weight is not only emotional. It is structural, interpretive, and temporal.

The claim can be reframed around what is preserved. Continuation often appears to preserve investment. At the same time, it can preserve the very conditions that make reevaluation harder. Preservation is not neutral. Preservation can include preservation of narrowing. Preservation can include preservation of interpretive pressure. Preservation can include preservation of inherited assumptions.

This is not a rejection of commitment. Commitment can be coherent and necessary. The judgment draws a boundary between commitment and automatic continuation. Commitment can remain reflective. Automatic continuation can remain unexamined. The sentence addresses the second condition without dismissing the first.

Another restatement keeps the same meaning. The risk is not merely that continuation might fail. The risk is that continuation might continue to succeed in ways that prevent re-seeing. Partial success can stabilize an unstable frame. Intermittent reinforcement can sustain a costly slope. Sufficient functioning can postpone direct contact with underlying drift.

This is not paradox for its own sake. It is a description of mixed signals. The mixed signal is simple: the process works and the process costs. The process delivers and the process narrows. The process remains active and the process reduces optionality. Holding these pairs without premature resolution is part of the chapter's anchor.

The statement can be slowed further. Continuing is the risk means that the cost is not postponed outside the act. The cost is embedded in the continuation itself. It accrues as continuation continues. It accrues before an explicit outcome is declared. It accrues even while the surface still supports ordinary interpretations of stability.

This does not imply hidden doom. It implies hidden shaping. The language is about shape more than event. Shape can change without alarm. Shape can change without announcement. Shape can change while everyone involved remains sincere, attentive, and hardworking.

Another boundary removes a common misreading. The sentence is not an invitation to interpret every persistence as harm. It does not universalize suspicion. It names a possibility that becomes visible under repetition. It asks that repetition not be treated as proof in itself. It does not replace one absolute with another.

The same judgment can be cast as a distinction between motion and relation. Motion can continue while relation shifts. The relation between effort and effect can change without changing the visible fact of effort. The relation between commitment and choice can change without changing the visible fact of commitment. The risk is in these relation shifts, not in motion alone.

This is not explanatory closure. No single formula settles when continuation has crossed into risk production. The chapter does not offer that threshold as instruction. It anchors a vocabulary that resists simplified reassurance. It keeps the sentence open enough to remain accurate across slow variation.

The sentence can be echoed once more. Continuing is the risk. Not because continuation is dramatic. Not because continuation is immoral. Not because continuation is always mistaken. Because continuation can quietly alter the terms under which continuation is judged. Because continuation can make its own continuation increasingly difficult to question. Because continuation can make risk feel external while risk is being internally built.

Another echo, with different stress. Risk is not only what continuation faces. Risk is what continuation composes. Risk is not only before continuation. Risk is during continuation. Risk is not only after continuation. Risk is in the way continuation redefines what counts as acceptable before anything appears final.

This can be said without closure. The sentence remains a definition anchor, not a command. It remains a boundary against misreading, not a path to resolution. It remains a way of holding one difficult proposition in view: that continuation can be both understandable and risky, both functional and narrowing, both justified and structurally costly, without collapsing into a single moral conclusion.

And so the phrase keeps its distance. Continuing is the risk. The judgment stays there. It does not turn into a method. It does not turn into a warning slogan. It does not turn into a final answer. It remains a slow statement about what repetition can do before anyone notices that repetition has changed the ground.

Another restatement can be held in narrower terms. Risk here is a function of continued accommodation. Accommodation is not dramatic. Accommodation is incremental. Incremental accommodation can be rational locally and costly globally. The sentence keeps global cost in view while local rationality remains intact.

This is not anti-rational language. Local rationality is real. Local rationality can still compose a narrowing field when repeated without re-grounding. The claim is compositional. It concerns what sequences do, not what moments intend.

The same idea can be written as a drift definition. Continuation can drift criteria without declaring criterion change. Declared criteria may remain constant. Operative criteria can still move. The risk lies in operative drift beneath declared continuity.

Another boundary: The judgment is not that all continuity hides drift. It is that drift can hide inside continuity. The distinction matters. It prevents overgeneralization while preserving vigilance against one specific misreading.

Again in different words. The process can remain coherent in appearance while becoming expensive in option space. Option space does not vanish suddenly. Option space can thin by habitual reprioritization. Habitual reprioritization can feel like responsibility. Feeling responsible does not cancel structural thinning.

This is not advice to distrust responsibility. It is a reminder that responsibility language can coincide with narrowing. Coincidence is not accusation. Coincidence is descriptive. The anchor remains descriptive.

A slower phrasing: Continuation can teach the system what to expect. What is expected becomes what is normal. What is normal becomes what is tolerated. What is tolerated becomes what is difficult to question. The risk is embedded in this chain.

Another negation: This is not fatalism. The sentence does not claim inevitability of harm. It claims that harm can be incubated by ordinary repetition without explicit warning markers. Incubation is probabilistic, not absolute.

The judgment can also be framed as asymmetry. Benefits of continuation often appear near-term and legible. Costs of continuation often appear long-term and diffuse. Near-term legibility can dominate interpretation. Diffuse cost can remain uncounted while still accumulating.

This is not an accounting formula. It is a semantic correction. Legible benefit is not identical with total benefit. Diffuse cost is not identical with absent cost. The chapter stabilizes these distinctions.

Another boundary against simplification. The statement does not reduce life to binary outcomes. It does not frame continuation and stopping as opposing doctrines. It only denies neutrality to sustained continuation under changing conditions. Denial of neutrality is the anchor.

The sentence can be echoed through vocabulary shifts. Continuation can become self-justifying. Continuation can become self-protective. Continuation can become self-sealing. Self-sealing does not mean closed to all change. Self-sealing means resistant to frame-level challenge while permitting local adjustment.

This is not a critique of adaptation. Local adaptation can be intelligent. The risk appears when adaptation repeatedly preserves frame assumptions that are no longer examined. Preserved assumptions can quietly govern tolerance escalation.

Another restatement with emphasis on threshold creep. The line between acceptable and unacceptable can move without explicit renegotiation. Movement can be gradual enough to evade recognition. Recognition delay is part of risk formation. Late recognition increases reversal cost. Increased reversal cost reinforces continuation. The loop strengthens itself.

This does not require external coercion. Structural reinforcement can occur without command. Command is not necessary for narrowing. Repetition can perform the same function through normalized expectations.

Another boundary statement: No hero is needed for this pattern. No villain is needed. The sentence does not depend on character narratives. It depends on temporal accumulation and interpretive adaptation.

The same core in minimal language. Continuation modifies context. Modified context modifies judgment. Modified judgment modifies continuation. The cycle can proceed without explicit recognition. That unrecognized cycle is the named risk.

This is not a demand for immediate interpretation. Immediate interpretation can miss slow structure. The chapter keeps language intentionally repetitive so the structure remains visible after urgency fades. Repetition here is not redundancy for effect. It is anchoring against drift in reading.

Another phrasing through what is not being claimed. Not that every extension is error. Not that every commitment is trap. Not that every persistence is denial. Only that persistence itself can become a site where risk is produced, distributed, and normalized.

The sentence can be repeated as a restraint. Continuing is the risk. This does not close the question. It opens the correct level of question. Not whether continuation feels justified now, but what continuation is doing to the structure that defines justification over time.

Another boundary against pedagogical conversion. This anchor is not a lesson plan. It does not progress toward a takeaway. It does not culminate in a tool. Its function is narrower: prevent misinterpretation by repeating the same judgment across adjacent language forms.

The judgment again, with distance. Risk can be generated by what appears to prevent risk. Stability practices can produce fragility of tolerance. Consistency signals can mask option decay. Ordinary continuation can quietly author extraordinary constraint.

This remains unresolved on purpose. No final moral is attached. No concluding directive is offered. The sentence remains in suspension, because the condition it names is itself gradual, recursive, and not fully capturable by one closure move.

Continuing is the risk. The phrase remains active, not solved.

One last boundary keeps the anchor from flattening. This judgment is not an alarm signal. It is a calibration signal. Calibration does not command a move. Calibration redefines what a move is being made within. In that sense, continuing is the risk remains a statement about context production, not behavior prescription.

The phrase therefore remains deliberately unfinished. It does not end in directive form. It does not close into conclusion. It stays as definition: continuation can compose the very risk it claims to manage.

Chapter 2

When Effort Stops Being Additive

Most people are taught a simple relationship between effort and outcome. If you put more in, you get more out. If progress slows, you increase input. If something matters, you try harder.

This relationship feels intuitive because it works so often, especially early on. In school, extra practice usually leads to improvement. In new projects, additional hours often produce visible movement. When a system is small, flexible, and responsive, effort behaves almost like a multiplier.

But this relationship does not scale indefinitely.

There comes a point where additional effort stops adding. Not because effort becomes meaningless, but because the system receiving it has changed.

More time does not produce more movement. More attention does not reduce uncertainty. More care does not stabilize the outcome.

At first, this is difficult to notice. The actions look the same. The hours increase. The seriousness remains. From the outside, it still resembles commitment.

Internally, something feels different.

The work becomes heavier without becoming clearer. The feedback arrives later, or not at all. The same actions that once produced progress now produce maintenance at best.

This is not failure. Failure is loud. Failure declares itself.

This is quieter. This is effort continuing inside a structure that no longer compounds it.

When effort is additive, each unit builds on the last. When effort stops being additive, each unit merely replaces what decays.

The problem is not that effort has stopped working. The problem is that effort is now preserving a state instead of moving it.

Most people interpret this moment incorrectly. They do not think the structure has changed. They think they have not tried hard enough.

So they add more.

They stay later. They focus harder. They optimize details. They remove distractions. They double down on seriousness.

From the inside, this feels responsible. From the outside, it looks like discipline.

But structurally, nothing shifts.

The system absorbs the effort without producing leverage. The additional input does not stack. It only sustains.

Over time, this creates a specific distortion.

The person feels increasingly invested. The outcome feels increasingly static. The distance between effort and result grows, but because the effort is real, the gap is hard to name.

It does not feel like stagnation. It feels like commitment that has not paid off yet.

This is the danger point.

Because effort still feels meaningful, continuing feels justified.

And because continuing feels justified, the structure is never questioned.

The longer this continues, the more effort becomes evidence against stopping.

Not because stopping is wrong, but because so much has already been put in.

Eventually, effort is no longer a tool. It becomes an anchor.

And the system remains unchanged.

In one setting, the shift appears in a project that once rewarded intensity. Early milestones came quickly, and the team could draw a direct line between late nights and visible output. A revised draft produced immediate comments, an extra review prevented obvious defects, and a weekend sprint moved a date that everyone could see on the board. Months later, the same gestures remain in place, but their effect is harder to locate. The board still updates, messages still circulate, and calendars still fill, yet each added hour seems to replace slippage that arrived earlier in the same day.

At first the pattern is interpreted as temporary congestion. People note that the season is dense, that dependencies are unusually complex, that other groups are delayed. They continue in the same posture because the language of temporary strain is familiar and socially acceptable. In status calls, there is no clear signal of breakdown. Items close, new items open, and nothing dramatic interrupts continuity. The rhythm looks intact from a distance. Up close, the sequence has changed: completion is followed by immediate erosion, and maintenance consumes the same energy once associated with progress.

A similar structure appears in personal administration, where a person tries to regain control by increasing attention. The inbox is sorted more often, notifications are cleared faster, and small obligations are answered before they age. The surface looks orderly for short intervals. By late afternoon, the order has thinned again. New requests arrive at the rate of response, then slightly faster. What felt like recovery in the morning is neutralized by evening. The next day begins with the same intention, and the same narrow gain dissolves across ordinary traffic.

Because effort is visible, the mind keeps searching for the hidden leverage point. Perhaps the problem is sequencing. Perhaps concentration has been diluted. Perhaps a stronger boundary around interruptions would restore compounding. These possibilities are considered repeatedly, often before sleep, often while moving between tasks. None of them is fully dismissed, and none of them changes the observed ratio between input and movement. The hesitation before judgment can last for weeks because each day offers a small example that seems to support either interpretation.

In operational work, non-additive effort often appears as constant correction. A process that once tolerated minor variation now requires supervision at every step. A missed detail no longer remains local; it propagates through connected systems and reappears in places far from the original event. Additional attention prevents escalation, but the prevention must be repeated continuously. The same person who prevented yesterday's issue must prevent a similar issue today, then again tomorrow. Effort remains useful, yet usefulness has narrowed into containment.

Another scene takes place in a household where coordination grows denser over time. Schedules are aligned each week with care, reminders are set, transport is arranged, and conflicts are resolved before they become visible disagreements. The household appears functional and even calm. Underneath, the coordinator notices that planning now serves to keep complexity flat rather than to create extra space. Free time is not expanding. It is being preserved against drift. Each act of attention prevents a small collapse of timing, and the prevention expires quickly.

The internal experience of this phase is rarely dramatic. There is no decisive moment when someone announces that effort has stopped compounding. Instead, awareness arrives in fragments. A task completed on Tuesday needs to be repeated on Thursday with no intervening change. A careful conversation settles a tension that returns in nearly identical form after a brief pause. A document finalized last month requires another full pass because surrounding conditions moved. Each instance can be explained alone. Together they form a slow pattern.

When people discuss this pattern with peers, language often protects continuity. They say things are "busy," "dynamic," or "in a heavy cycle." These descriptions are not inaccurate, but they avoid naming the structural change. Naming would require admitting that more input is no longer producing more capacity. Without that admission, the default response is to supply additional input. Extra effort appears prudent, and prudence preserves identity. The person remains serious, responsible, and engaged, even while leverage continues to thin.

In institutional contexts, leaders can also misread the condition. They observe teams working harder and interpret the visible exertion as momentum. Reports show high activity, response times remain acceptable, and stakeholders receive steady communication. Since work is occurring everywhere, the assumption is that progress is being made everywhere. The distinction between movement and stabilization is easy to miss in aggregate metrics. Local contributors feel the distinction directly, but the texture of that feeling rarely appears in dashboards.

Time deepens the distortion. After several months, the accumulated investment itself becomes evidence that continuation is necessary. People reason that because so much has been committed, the current stage must be close to turning. The same reasoning appears in small and large domains: a long product cycle, a prolonged hiring process, a difficult renovation, a relationship under strain. In each case, prior effort is treated as a signal about future return. Sometimes this signal is accurate. In non-additive conditions, it is often only a record of persistence.

Hesitation remains present because the system never becomes entirely unresponsive. Small wins still occur. A week arrives with fewer disruptions. A specific intervention prevents a known problem. A conversation lands more cleanly than expected. These moments are real, and they complicate judgment. If progress were absent, the structure would be easier to name. Instead there is intermittent reinforcement, enough to sustain belief that compounding may resume if intensity is maintained a little longer.

The delayed realization tends to unfold through comparison rather than revelation. Someone looks back at two periods with similar effort and notices that one produced expansion while the other produced continuity. The observation is quiet and often private. It may occur while reviewing old notes, scanning archived messages, or remembering how the same work once felt. No immediate decision follows. The recognition simply remains, recurring at odd times, competing with the daily imperative to keep inputs high.

Across contexts, the repeated structure is plain: action is added, degradation is offset, baseline is preserved, and the cycle restarts.

The loop can run for a long time because each component appears rational on its own. Nothing looks obviously wasteful in isolation. Only the aggregate view reveals that effort has shifted from building to holding. Even then, language resists finality. People continue to describe the phase as transitional, temporary, or unusually demanding, and those descriptions remain plausible.

In this state, seriousness is not absent. Care is not absent. Skill is not absent. What changes is the exchange rate between exertion and directional change. The person at the center can feel that rate changing before they can explain it. They notice that finishing one thing no longer clears space for the next. They notice that rest creates backlog instead of recovery. They notice that intensity produces fewer surprises, not more possibility. The observations accumulate without closing into a verdict.

Days continue in recognizable form. Meetings occur, messages are answered, repairs are made, and promises are kept. From outside, the pattern resembles commitment under pressure. From inside, the pressure is not only volume; it is the absence of stacking. Each added unit of work lands, does its local job, and expires. Another unit is required to maintain the same contour. The arrangement can persist indefinitely, appearing stable while consuming progressively more attention.

No singular event marks the threshold. The threshold is inferred after many repetitions, often reluctantly. Even then, people may keep testing the old equation, adding effort to see whether leverage returns. Sometimes the test extends longer than expected because the structure still permits partial gains. The day ends with tasks completed and little directional shift. The next day begins with the same intention, the same seriousness, and the same uncertain ratio between work and movement.

In a technical operations context, the same non-additive pattern appears during incident management cycles. Teams respond faster, document better, and monitor more channels, yet the total effort required to keep service quality steady grows each quarter. Improvements prevent obvious failures, but the prevention does not free capacity. Capacity is consumed by the next layer of preventative work. The system appears mature from outside because outage headlines are rare. Inside the team, maturity is experienced as continuous vigilance that preserves baseline reliability rather than creating cumulative margin.

In education, instructors can encounter a parallel loop. Additional preparation, closer feedback, and more careful communication improve daily classroom stability, but they do not always create long-term reduction in workload. Each semester begins with refined materials and ends with comparable fatigue. Refinements are useful and visible, yet they mostly counter new variability in student needs, policy shifts, and administrative demands. The net effect feels flat. Work remains meaningful while leverage remains limited.

Another delayed realization occurs when historical comparisons are made informally. A person remembers earlier periods when similar effort yielded new room: less rework, fewer clarifications, more durable outcomes. In the current period, similar effort yields recurrence: repeated fixes, repeated alignment, repeated verification. The person does not immediately trust this comparison. Memory can simplify the past. Still, the comparison returns repeatedly and begins to feel less like nostalgia and more like structural observation.

Across these examples, the day still contains completion events, and completion events still provide short bursts of confirmation. A task closes, a problem is contained, a conversation lands. Short confirmation makes the longer pattern difficult to confront because it supplies legitimate reasons to continue unchanged. Nothing about these moments is false. Their truth sits alongside another truth: each completion now decays quickly and must be renewed with similar effort. The coexistence of these truths sustains prolonged ambiguity.

As ambiguity persists, people often increase precision in local execution. They refine formatting, tighten handoffs, and improve follow-through. Precision can reduce noise and deserves respect. In non-additive conditions, however, reduced noise does not necessarily restore compounding. The system may simply absorb higher-quality input while preserving the same exchange rate between effort and directional change. The person feels increasingly exact and increasingly stationary at once, a combination that is difficult to name in real time.

Months later, the pattern may still be unresolved. Work continues with care, and outcomes remain acceptable, yet the sense of stacking remains absent. The person can identify many useful actions and still question whether usefulness has narrowed into repeated preservation. No definitive event settles the question. The chapter extends through ordinary weeks where added effort remains real, necessary, and only partially cumulative.

Another unresolved scene appears at quarter boundaries. Teams review output volume and notice that activity stayed high while expansion indicators stayed flat. No one disputes the amount of work completed. The open question is why completed work no longer clears future capacity. Discussion circles through staffing, tooling, coordination, and market timing, then returns to the next week's commitments before a shared interpretation settles. The cycle resumes with renewed effort and incomplete explanation.

In this ongoing pattern, each day still contains meaningful tasks and careful execution. What remains uncertain is whether meaning is now mostly local rather than cumulative. The uncertainty does not prevent continuation. It travels with continuation, resurfacing whenever effort is added and the system responds with preservation rather than additional room.

In everyday practice, this means effort remains continuous while interpretation remains provisional. The person can point to real contributions made each day and still remain unsure whether the system is being advanced or merely sustained. That uncertainty does not interrupt the workflow. It stays alongside it, returning whenever another completed cycle leaves the overall contour largely unchanged.

Chapter 3

When Continuation Becomes Protective

There is a moment when continuing stops feeling optional.

It does not arrive suddenly. Nothing dramatic announces it. No explicit demand is made.

Instead, the feeling shifts quietly. What once felt like a choice begins to feel like a responsibility. Pausing no longer feels neutral. Stepping back carries an undefined cost.

Most people notice this change indirectly. They feel tension when imagining a break. They hesitate before slowing down. Rest produces anxiety rather than relief.

This reaction is confusing because nothing obvious has gone wrong. The work may still be competent. The role may still be respected. The project may still appear viable.

From the outside, continuation looks reasonable. From the inside, it begins to feel protective.

Protection is different from progress. Progress moves toward something. Protection holds something together.

When continuation becomes protective, effort is no longer aimed at expansion. It is aimed at preventing loss. This loss may not be catastrophic. It may be subtle: credibility, momentum, coherence, trust.

The system does not threaten collapse. It threatens erosion.

Because erosion is gradual, protection feels justified. Each action prevents a small slide. Each response avoids a minor issue. Each presence reassures someone, including oneself.

Over time, this protective role becomes normalized. What began as attentiveness becomes vigilance. What began as care becomes monitoring.

The difference is not visible in outcomes. It is felt in posture.

Protective continuation requires constant awareness. Small deviations matter. Silence invites interpretation. Absence creates questions.

This posture is exhausting, but not obviously so. It does not resemble burnout. There may still be energy, interest, even pride.

What changes is the margin for error. The system now depends on continued alignment.

Many people misinterpret this dependence. They believe the increased pressure reflects importance. They assume that feeling needed is a sign of value.

In reality, dependence signals fragility. Not failure, but sensitivity.

A sensitive system reacts quickly to changes. It performs well under stable conditions. It struggles with disruption.

Protective continuation stabilizes such systems. It compensates for their sensitivity. It absorbs shocks before they register externally.

This compensation often goes unnoticed. Problems do not escalate. Conflicts remain manageable. Deadlines are met.

Success reinforces the pattern.

Each successful intervention confirms that presence matters. Each avoided issue suggests that absence would have caused harm. The system learns what it can rely on.

This learning is not conscious. It emerges through repetition.

Over time, protective continuation shifts expectations. Responses are assumed. Availability is normalized. Buffers shrink.

The system does not demand more explicitly. It simply reorganizes around what is consistently provided.

This is why stopping feels risky even when nothing appears broken. The risk is not failure. It is exposure.

Without protective effort, sensitivities become visible. Delays surface. Misalignments appear. Small cracks show.

None of these necessarily lead to collapse. But they break the illusion of stability.

For many people, this illusion is valuable. It supports identity. It maintains reputation. It preserves narrative continuity.

Protective continuation keeps the story intact.

This is where the trap forms. Not because continuing is wrong, but because stopping threatens to reveal what has been quietly held together.

The fear is not of collapse. It is of disclosure.

Disclosure can take many forms. Others may notice limitations. Assumptions may be questioned. Roles may shift.

These possibilities are rarely articulated. They exist as background tension rather than explicit scenarios.

Because the risk is undefined, it is difficult to evaluate. It feels safer to continue than to test what would happen otherwise.

Protective continuation thrives on this ambiguity. As long as the cost of stopping remains unclear, continuing appears prudent.

This prudence is reinforced socially. Responsiveness is praised. Reliability is rewarded. Consistency is framed as professionalism or commitment.

Rarely does anyone ask what is being protected. The assumption is that protection itself is virtuous.

But protection is not neutral. It preserves existing arrangements. It delays adaptation. It hides structural limits.

Again, this does not make it wrong. It makes it consequential.

Protective continuation gradually shifts responsibility. The system no longer carries itself. It leans.

This leaning is subtle. No single moment establishes it. No contract defines it.

Yet it becomes real through repetition.

Once leaning exists, absence feels heavier. The system does not fail without you, but it becomes visibly less smooth.

That visibility creates discomfort. Not necessarily for others, but for the person who notices it.

Many people remain in protective continuation not because they are forced, but because they are aware of what they are holding.

They know, even vaguely, that stepping back would change the texture of things. They sense that ease would be replaced by friction.

This awareness creates obligation. Not moral obligation, but structural obligation.

You stay because leaving would require reconfiguration. You continue because stopping would reveal dependency.

Protective continuation is difficult to exit cleanly. Not because exit is impossible, but because there is no obvious signal that permission has been granted.

The system does not say "you may stop." It has adapted to your presence.

Understanding this does not instruct anyone to leave. It does not argue for disruption. It does not frame protection as a mistake.

It simply clarifies why continuation can feel heavy even when nothing is explicitly wrong.

When continuation becomes protective, the question is no longer about effort. It is about what effort is shielding, and what would become visible without it.

This visibility is often the true source of perceived risk.

In one organization, continuation becomes protective during a period with no visible crisis. Deliverables still ship, customers still receive responses, and leadership updates still project steadiness. Inside the workflow, however, certain people begin to carry a silent buffering role. They answer questions before confusion spreads, adjust language before disagreements harden, and re-sequence tasks before timing conflicts are noticed by others. The day remains orderly partly because these adjustments occur continuously. Protection is distributed through small acts that rarely appear in formal records.

At first this buffering is interpreted as professionalism. The person who notices a gap and closes it is praised for reliability. The person who stays available after hours is described as committed. Over time, the praise itself changes the structure. What began as occasional intervention becomes expected presence. The system learns that instability can be absorbed if this person remains attentive. There is no explicit handoff of responsibility. The dependency forms through repetition and successful avoidance of visible friction.

A similar dynamic appears in family life when one member tracks the emotional weather of the household. They adjust tone before conflict grows, smooth scheduling tension before it becomes argument, and carry information between people who are too tired to coordinate directly. Nothing dramatic is prevented; instead, many small escalations never materialize. Because the prevented events do not occur, their prevention is difficult to measure. The household feels normal, and normality disguises how much active stabilization is being supplied.

Protective continuation often includes a constant preview of potential disruption. In meetings, a person listens not only for current content but for secondary effects that might appear later. A loose phrase could trigger confusion in another team. A delayed approval could expose an upstream deadline. A missed acknowledgment could alter trust. The person intervenes early, and the predicted disruption remains hypothetical. This reinforces the belief that continued vigilance is necessary, even when no one else can verify what was avoided.

Hesitation before judgment takes a particular form here. The person wonders whether their presence is truly essential or merely habitual. They imagine stepping back and picture minor disorder that might resolve on its own. They also imagine small failures cascading into reputational cost for others. Neither scenario is fully convincing. The ambiguity favors continuation because continuation keeps the question unresolved. As long as protection continues, the counterfactual remains inaccessible.

In institutional settings, protective continuation can be mistaken for strategic excellence. Leadership may notice that one unit consistently absorbs late changes without visible disruption. The unit earns trust and receives additional load. New work is routed there because outcomes remain smooth. What appears as high capability is partly high compensation. The team is not only executing tasks; it is preventing system sensitivities from becoming public. This hidden function expands without being named as a function.

The same structure appears in friendship networks. One person remembers birthdays, coordinates gatherings, translates misunderstandings, and notices when someone is quietly withdrawing. The group stays cohesive in part because this labor persists. If the person pauses for a few weeks, nothing collapses, yet the texture changes. Messages become less frequent, assumptions go uncorrected, and invitations thin. The shift is subtle enough to be explained as busy schedules, which allows the protective role to remain invisible even during brief absence.

Protection also modifies time perception. Days are filled with small interventions that each feel necessary and brief. At the end of the week, there is little visible progress to report, yet there is a strong sense of having worked continuously. This mismatch can be disorienting. Effort has been substantial, but its product is the non-appearance of problems. Non-events do not accumulate into obvious milestones. They accumulate into a maintained baseline that appears natural to everyone who benefits from it.

As continuation becomes protective, language shifts toward obligation without explicit command. People say, "It helps when you're around," or "Things run smoother when you're here." These statements are descriptive, not coercive, but their effect is similar. Presence becomes linked to collective stability. Absence becomes linked to risk, even if the risk remains undefined. The person absorbing this message may agree partly, doubt partly, and continue anyway because uncertainty makes withdrawal feel imprudent.

Delay in realization often comes from successful adaptation. Because crises are avoided, there is no clear trigger for reevaluation. If visible failure occurred, roles might be renegotiated. Instead, visible failure is minimized, so renegotiation appears unnecessary. Months pass under this arrangement. The person who stabilizes the system may sense growing heaviness without a corresponding incident to point to. Heaviness alone feels insufficient as evidence, so continuation persists while interpretation lags.

Across domains, protective continuation narrows the margin for spontaneity. Plans can still change, but only if someone absorbs the resulting disorder in real time. The absorber gradually loses unstructured space, then treats this loss as ordinary. Their availability is no longer seen as extra; it is assumed in planning. Others schedule with that assumption, speak with that assumption, and commit with that assumption. No policy states this dependency. Practice establishes it and normalizes it.

The internal posture during this phase is often alert but not panicked. There is attention to early signals, quick adjustments, and low tolerance for unresolved ambiguity. This posture can feel competent and even satisfying in short bursts. Over long periods it becomes background strain. Strain remains difficult to name because outcomes are acceptable. The person is not failing publicly. They are preserving coherence privately, then repeating the preservation before the previous cycle has fully settled.

Protective continuation also affects identity. Being the one who keeps things together becomes part of how others describe the person and how the person describes themselves. Identity stabilizes behavior. When stepping back is imagined, the concern is not only operational disruption but symbolic disruption: who am I in this system if I no longer absorb these shocks? The question rarely receives a direct answer. It lingers as unease, and unease supports continued presence.

In teams, turnover can expose the pattern indirectly. A stabilizing member takes leave, and peers notice that handoffs become rougher, communications slower, and minor conflicts more visible. None of these outcomes is catastrophic. Still, their emergence reveals how much smoothing had been supplied continuously. When the person returns, smoothness returns quickly, and the episode is narrated as a temporary rough patch rather than evidence of structural dependence. The narrative protects continuity and postpones deeper judgment.

Scene follows scene with similar geometry: a small disruption appears, a protective response absorbs it, visible order remains, and the response is forgotten. The loop repeats in different costumes across work, home, and community contexts. Each loop strengthens the intuition that continuation is necessary for stability. The intuition may be partly accurate. It may also be self-reinforcing, since continued protection prevents the system from displaying its own adaptation capacity.

Over longer periods, the unresolved question is not whether protection is good or bad. The unresolved question is what exactly is being held in place and what would shift if that holding loosened. The answer is rarely immediate. People continue through ordinary weeks, maintain ordinary conversations, and manage ordinary interruptions while that question remains in the background. The structure stays intact, and continuation retains its protective function without reaching a final explanation.

Protective continuation can also appear in client-facing roles where one person continually translates between internal constraints and external expectations. They adjust wording to prevent alarm, manage timing to prevent escalation, and absorb dissatisfaction before it spreads. Outcomes appear stable, so stakeholders assume the system itself is stable. The stabilizing labor remains attached to one person's sustained attention. If that attention briefly thins, small tensions surface quickly, then are reabsorbed when attentiveness returns.

In long-running collaborations, participants may sense this dependency without naming it. They describe one member as "central" or "indispensable," then continue routing delicate situations through that member. The routing solves immediate coordination problems and postpones structural redesign. Everyone benefits from the short-term smoothness. The long-term question of what is being protected stays unexamined, not because it is forbidden, but because daily operations keep rewarding the current arrangement.

Another scene is temporal: after a short absence, the protective person returns and notices accumulated micro-frictions that others treated as normal variation. They clear the friction in a few focused hours. The quick recovery can be interpreted as proof that the system is fundamentally sound. It can also be interpreted as proof that hidden buffering remains necessary. Both interpretations remain available, and continuation proceeds with the question unresolved.

Across these repetitions, protection is sustained through ordinary acts that leave little trace. No resolution arrives. The system remains coherent, dependency remains partly visible, and continuation keeps feeling like the prudent way to avoid exposing what has been quietly held together.

The protective phase can persist even when everyone involved is thoughtful and cooperative. Stability remains visible, minor disruptions keep getting absorbed, and no clear moment demands redesign. As a result, continuation continues to feel safer than exposure, and exposure continues to feel unnecessary as long as immediate functioning remains intact.

Protection remains active under ordinary conditions, and ordinary conditions keep masking how active it is. The structure stays coherent, the buffering continues, and the question of what would happen without that buffering remains unanswered.

Chapter 4

How Risk Quietly Expands

When continuation becomes protective, risk begins to feel larger than it used to.

This expansion rarely reflects objective danger. It is not the appearance of new threats. It is the amplification of sensitivity.

What once felt tolerable now feels exposed. What once seemed manageable now feels fragile.

Importantly, this shift does not require failure. In fact, it often happens precisely because things are still working.

When systems operate smoothly, their tolerance for disruption decreases. Small variations stand out. Minor inconsistencies attract attention.

The system becomes quieter, and in that quiet, every disturbance sounds louder.

This is how perceived risk expands without any corresponding change in reality.

Early on, uncertainty is absorbed. Mistakes blend into learning. Delays are contextualized as part of progress.

Later, the same events feel heavier. A missed response carries meaning. A delay suggests decline. An absence invites interpretation.

Nothing objectively worse has occurred. But interpretation density has increased.

This density is not arbitrary. It is produced by structure.

Protective continuation reduces slack. Buffers shrink. Redundancies disappear.

The system becomes efficient, and efficiency trades resilience for precision.

Precision demands consistency. Consistency demands vigilance.

As vigilance increases, the system's tolerance narrows.

This narrowing creates a feedback loop. The more carefully the system is maintained, the more sensitive it becomes to lapses.

Each avoided issue confirms the need for attention. Each intervention prevents evidence that the system might cope on its own.

Over time, the absence of problems is no longer reassuring. It becomes dependent on continued presence.

Risk perception grows in this environment. Not because danger has increased, but because deviation has become visible.

This is why people often feel that stopping is dangerous even when they cannot articulate the danger.

The risk is not collapse. It is loss of smoothness. Loss of coherence. Loss of narrative control.

These losses are subtle, but they matter to systems that have become finely tuned.

Fine-tuned systems do not fail loudly. They degrade quietly.

A small misalignment spreads. A delay compounds. Uncertainty lingers.

Protective continuation masks these effects. It absorbs them before they propagate.

Removing that protection reveals the system's true tolerance. This revelation feels risky, not because it introduces new problems, but because it exposes existing limits.

Exposure is uncomfortable. It interrupts the story that everything is under control.

Many people respond to this discomfort by increasing effort further. They tighten monitoring. They shorten response times. They reduce absence even more.

This response is understandable. It restores the familiar sense of control.

But it also accelerates the loop. As control increases, tolerance decreases further.

Risk perception grows again.

Eventually, the idea of stopping feels disproportionate to any observable benefit. The cost is imagined as catastrophic, even if evidence suggests otherwise.

This is not delusion. It is pattern recognition applied to a sensitive system.

The system has learned to rely on continuity. Risk is now defined relative to that reliance.

Importantly, this reliance is rarely mutual. The system may not consciously acknowledge dependence. Others may not articulate expectation.

Yet the structure behaves as if reliance exists.

This asymmetry deepens risk perception. You sense that your absence would matter, but you are not certain how or to whom.

Uncertainty magnifies perceived risk. Undefined consequences feel larger than defined ones.

Because the risk is vague, it cannot be easily evaluated. Because it cannot be evaluated, it cannot be dismissed.

Continuation becomes the safer option by default.

This default is reinforced by time. The longer protection continues, the more the system adapts to it. The more it adapts, the greater the imagined cost of withdrawal.

Risk expands quietly, fed by adaptation rather than threat.

Understanding this does not eliminate risk. It does not guarantee safety. It does not justify exit.

It clarifies why risk can feel overwhelming without any specific danger being present.

When risk grows without shape, it becomes persuasive. Not because it is accurate, but because it cannot be disproven.

This is the environment in which continuation begins to feel inevitable.

Not because stopping is impossible, but because the risk of stopping has grown larger than the system itself.

From a distance, this pattern is easier to see in systems that appear calm for long stretches. A team can go months without major disruption, and in that period every small variance starts receiving more interpretation than before. A late reply is read as a possible signal. A minor handoff error is treated as evidence of fragility. Nothing in the event itself has changed; what has changed is the interpretive weight attached to ordinary variation. Observers looking across quarters notice that the same types of incidents were once absorbed with little discussion, then later discussed with increasing seriousness, while objective incident volume remains nearly flat.

In institutional settings, this expanded risk perception tends to follow long runs of successful smoothing. Coordinators, managers, and informal stabilizers keep small issues contained so consistently that the organization stops seeing those issues as normal background noise. The baseline is reset to near-frictionless operation. Once that baseline is established, even routine irregularity can look exceptional. The pattern repeats in different sectors: service teams, research groups, nonprofit operations, and households with dense logistics.

The surface message remains the same everywhere: we cannot afford disruption now, even when the measurable environment has not become more dangerous.

Time delay makes the shift difficult to name in real time. Participants inside the system often describe the period as simply "more sensitive" without identifying when sensitivity expanded. Looking back, the sequence appears gradual: buffers are tightened, response times shorten, backup capacity is treated as inefficiency, and tolerance narrows step by step. Each change looks reasonable in isolation. The cumulative effect appears only later, when people notice that perceived risk has grown faster than external threat. The recognition comes after adaptation, not before it.

Third-party observers also notice asymmetry between what is feared and what is discussed. The language of risk becomes broad and continuous, while specific failure models remain vague. People talk about things becoming risky, but struggle to define which concrete event is now newly catastrophic. This vagueness does not weaken perception; it strengthens it. Undefined risk is harder to calibrate, so it remains active in the background. A system can therefore feel increasingly endangered while producing no corresponding map of new danger.

Across repeated cycles, the system-level effect is consistent: continuation reduces visible disturbance, reduced disturbance increases perceived cost of disturbance, and perceived cost justifies tighter continuation. The loop can run quietly for years. From the inside, it feels like responsible maintenance. From the outside, it resembles a structural narrowing of tolerance. Neither view needs to cancel the other. Both can describe the same period from different distances.

Over longer windows, analysts often find that major outcomes changed less than expected while attention patterns changed substantially. More time is spent preventing interpretive disruption, less time is spent testing tolerance directly, and absence of visible failure is treated as proof that current vigilance is indispensable. The chapter remains open in that condition: risk feels large, threats remain partly undefined, and the system continues adapting around a sensitivity that grew gradually enough to feel natural.

A broader operational view also shows how expanded risk perception can be maintained by reporting habits. When teams move into protection mode, they often increase frequency of status checks and exception tracking. The additional visibility is useful, but it also changes what the group experiences as normal. More checkpoints create more moments where slight irregularities can be noticed and labeled. Over time, the volume of labels can rise even if material conditions are stable. Participants then encounter a constant stream of minor caution signals and infer that overall exposure has increased, when part of the increase is observational intensity.

In service environments, this pattern repeats across shifts. One team inherits a stable process with low incident rates and introduces tighter controls to preserve quality. A second team, seeing the tighter controls and frequent alerts, interprets the system as inherently fragile. A third team inherits that interpretation and treats ordinary variation as high-salience risk. None of the teams is acting irrationally. Each team is responding to the operational context it can see. The cumulative effect is a culture where threat language intensifies across time while external volatility remains modest.

Long-range review usually reveals that confidence and sensitivity moved in opposite directions. Systems became better at avoiding visible errors and less comfortable with testing tolerance. Small pauses, temporary absences, and imperfect handoffs were treated less as routine stress tests and more as unacceptable deviations. This reduced opportunity to observe the system coping without intervention. Without those observations, participants had fewer data points showing that resilience still existed. Perceived risk expanded partly through missing evidence of ordinary recoverability.

From a portfolio perspective, multiple units can display the same curve at once. Units that maintain high smoothness begin to share similar language about narrow margins and non-negotiable continuity. Their outcomes differ, but their risk posture converges. External reviewers often note that this convergence emerges without coordinated policy. It grows through repeated local decisions that favor predictability and suppress visible fluctuation. The result is a distributed environment where many actors independently conclude that interruption is unusually dangerous.

The repeated system pattern remains quiet and self-reinforcing: more stabilization creates higher expectations of stabilization, higher expectations amplify perception of deviation, amplified deviation perception justifies more stabilization. The cycle does not require explicit fear narratives to persist. It can run through normal planning, normal communication, and normal accountability practices, while the felt size of risk continues to grow relative to the underlying event landscape.

Another long-view observation concerns what gets archived and what gets forgotten. Systems tend to retain records of incidents and interventions, but rarely retain records of uneventful tolerance. Over time, archives become dense with examples of what almost went wrong and thin on examples of what remained stable without extra action. Later readers of those archives encounter an imbalance and infer that exposure has been steadily rising. The inference is understandable and often incomplete.

As this archival imbalance repeats across planning cycles, participants inherit a risk story with high detail on potential disruption and low detail on ordinary recoverability. This story influences language, pacing, and staffing even when external variance remains limited. The system keeps operating, and perceived fragility continues to expand through documentation patterns as much as through direct experience.

Seen across even longer timelines, the same system can pass through several leadership periods, staffing mixes, and external conditions while preserving this heightened perception pattern. New participants inherit an environment where small disruptions are already interpreted through a narrow tolerance lens, and they adapt quickly to that lens because it appears to be evidence-based. They see dense monitoring, frequent micro-escalation protocols, and careful continuity practices, then assume these arrangements were built in response to escalating external hazard. Sometimes that assumption is correct; sometimes the arrangements were largely endogenous, created by prior successful stabilization. The distinction is difficult to establish because the system now produces data through the very tools that encode its sensitivity. In that setting, ordinary variance is repeatedly converted into structured signal, structured signal is repeatedly treated as confirmation of exposure, and confirmation is repeatedly used to justify further sensitivity. The mechanism is procedural, not dramatic. It unfolds through routine planning documents, routine staffing conversations, and routine quality checks. Participants remain serious and competent throughout. What changes is the range of disturbance considered tolerable before interpretive alarm is triggered, and that range can continue narrowing quietly long after external conditions have stopped changing in meaningful ways.

This leaves a system that can look externally steady while internally calibrating itself to ever smaller deviations, with risk language expanding by iteration rather than by singular event.

Chapter 5

When Continuing Starts to Feel Like the Right Thing

At a certain point, continuation stops being a practical choice and begins to feel morally correct.

This shift is subtle. No one declares it. No rule announces it.

Yet the feeling is real.

Continuing begins to carry a sense of virtue. It signals responsibility. It suggests commitment. It implies strength.

Stopping, by contrast, feels questionable. It invites scrutiny. It requires explanation.

This imbalance does not emerge because stopping is wrong. It emerges because continuation has accumulated meaning.

That meaning is not inherent. It is produced.

Early on, effort is functional. It solves problems. It advances progress. It responds to opportunity.

Later, when effort becomes protective, its visibility increases. People notice presence. They notice reliability. They notice consistency.

These qualities are socially legible. They are easy to praise.

Reliability becomes a character trait. Consistency becomes an identity. Responsiveness becomes proof of care.

None of this is false. But none of it is neutral.

As these traits are reinforced, continuation absorbs moral weight. To continue is not just to act, but to demonstrate something about oneself.

This demonstration rarely feels performative. It feels sincere. People internalize the values they are rewarded for.

Over time, the question changes. It is no longer "Does this make sense?" It becomes "What does it say if I stop?"

This is where judgment begins to blur.

Stopping is no longer evaluated structurally. It is evaluated symbolically. It suggests withdrawal. It hints at failure. It risks being interpreted as avoidance.

These interpretations are not always voiced. Often, they are anticipated.

Anticipation is enough.

The imagined reactions of others become part of the decision environment. The internal dialogue shifts.

Continuing feels clean. Stopping feels messy.

This cleanliness is appealing. It simplifies self-understanding. It aligns action with identity.

Once continuation is morally charged, questioning it feels destabilizing. It threatens coherence.

Many people avoid this threat by reframing discomfort as fatigue rather than misalignment.

They tell themselves they need rest, not reevaluation. They plan short breaks instead of structural pauses.

This strategy works temporarily. It reduces strain without challenging meaning. Continuation resumes intact.

Over time, however, the gap between effort and clarity widens. The work continues, but understanding lags.

This lag is uncomfortable, yet it remains unnamed. To name it would require separating value from action.

That separation is difficult once continuation has been moralized.

Importantly, this moralization does not require pressure from others. Often, it is self-generated.

People hold themselves to standards they believe they represent. They continue because that is who they are.

This identity-based continuation is resilient. It survives doubt. It absorbs critique. It reframes misalignment as personal weakness.

The danger here is not exhaustion. It is confusion.

When continuation carries moral weight, judgment loses neutrality. Evaluation becomes biased toward staying.

Evidence is filtered. Costs are minimized. Alternatives are dismissed prematurely.

This bias does not feel dishonest. It feels loyal.

Loyalty to roles. Loyalty to narratives. Loyalty to past effort.

These loyalties are powerful. They stabilize behavior. They reduce uncertainty.

But they also reduce visibility.

Once continuation is framed as the right thing, the space for genuine evaluation shrinks. Questioning feels like betrayal. Doubt feels indulgent.

This is how people remain in situations long after structural alignment has faded.

Not because they cannot leave, but because leaving would contradict the story they have been living.

Understanding this does not invalidate commitment. It does not accuse anyone of self-deception. It simply shows how meaning accumulates.

Continuation feels right because it has been made right.

That feeling deserves examination, not obedience.

Without examination, judgment quietly defers to identity.

And identity, once engaged, is very difficult to argue with.

In some environments, continuation gains moral weight through repetition rather than argument. A person keeps showing up under difficult conditions, keeps answering when others are silent, keeps handling unfinished work that no one explicitly owns. Over time, observers stop describing these actions as practical responses and begin describing them as character. The behavior is interpreted as proof of seriousness. The interpretation circulates in ordinary remarks, performance reviews, and private conversations. What began as situational effort is gradually translated into a stable description of who this person is.

Once this translation occurs, hesitation appears in a new form. Doubt about continuation is no longer only doubt about strategy; it becomes doubt about identity. The person wonders whether stepping back would be interpreted as inconsistency, weakness, or withdrawal of care. No one may say these words aloud. Their possibility is enough to alter judgment. Continuing feels clean because it preserves coherence between past behavior and current role. Stopping feels noisy because it introduces interpretive uncertainty.

A parallel pattern appears in caregiving contexts. Someone manages appointments, medication logistics, and daily checks over a long period. Family members express gratitude and admiration, often sincerely. Admiration can harden into expectation. If the caregiver considers reducing involvement, the imagined reaction is not merely logistical concern but moral confusion: why reduce now, after being so dependable for so long? The question remains unasked in many families, yet it shapes behavior through anticipation.

Moralization can also develop in professional teams where one contributor repeatedly rescues deadlines. At first the rescue is exceptional. Later it is assumed. Colleagues frame the person as the one who always carries critical moments. Praise accompanies this framing, and praise feels validating. At the same time, the framing narrows acceptable behavior. Declining another rescue appears less like boundary-setting and more like abandonment of a trusted role. The social meaning attached to continuation grows heavier with every successful intervention.

Internal dialogue changes slowly. Early reasoning focuses on utility: this task matters, this phase is temporary, this effort solves a concrete problem. Later reasoning focuses on symbolism: this is what responsible people do, this is how commitment is demonstrated, this is what consistency looks like. The shift may go unnoticed because both forms of reasoning can be true at once. Utility and symbolism overlap. The overlap makes it difficult to tell when continuation is being sustained for outcomes and when it is being sustained for identity maintenance.

Scene after scene repeats the same structure in different settings. In a volunteer group, one member handles tedious coordination month after month because nobody else can do it as smoothly. In a research collaboration, one investigator continues a weak line of inquiry because leaving now would look like disloyalty to years of collective work. In a small business, an owner extends unprofitable services because withdrawing them feels like betraying long-term clients. The contexts differ, but the moral pressure around continuation is similar.

Temporal delay matters here. Moral meanings accumulate gradually and often become visible only in hindsight. A person reviewing old correspondence may notice how language evolved from "thanks for helping" to "we count on you for this." The change occurred over many small exchanges, none of which seemed consequential at the time. Once the new language is established, decisions are interpreted through it. Continuation confirms the role; deviation requires explanation that feels disproportionate to the specific choice at hand.

Hesitation before judgment can stretch for months because evidence points both ways. Continuation still produces some useful results. Others still benefit. Identity still feels coherent when the pattern is maintained. At the same time, the person notices a narrowing of options and a growing reluctance to evaluate alternatives openly. These observations do not cancel the value of commitment. They coexist with it, creating a dense decision environment where moral and structural signals are difficult to separate.

In many institutions, policies indirectly reinforce this dynamic. Reliability is rewarded in promotion decisions, while discontinuity is examined for hidden risk. Narratives of perseverance are celebrated in retrospectives and internal communications. These practices are understandable, yet they can unintentionally frame continuation as the ethically superior default. Individuals internalize the frame and pre-filter their own judgments accordingly. They do not feel coerced. They feel aligned with what the environment recognizes as honorable.

The moral framing becomes self-sustaining when peers rely on it to make predictions. People assign tasks based on who is "the dependable one." They share concerns with who is "always there." Planning assumptions follow these labels. The labeled person receives more opportunities to continue and fewer opportunities to pause without social interpretation. Continuation remains voluntary in principle, but in practice it is woven into collective expectation. Voluntary and expected begin to overlap until the distinction becomes difficult to experience.

Another recurrent scene is private and quiet: late at night, the person imagines not continuing and immediately rehearses how that choice would be narrated by others. Even supportive peers are imagined asking for reasons. Reasons are available, yet each one sounds incomplete when compared with the simple moral clarity of continued effort. The imagined conversation becomes an argument for postponement. No definitive judgment is reached. Morning arrives, obligations resume, and continuation proceeds with renewed justification.

When continuation is moralized, discomfort often gets interpreted as personal deficiency rather than structural signal. Fatigue means insufficient discipline. Ambivalence means insufficient gratitude. Friction means insufficient resilience. These interpretations are not always explicit; they appear as tone and self-evaluation rather than formal conclusions. Because the frame is moral, structural analysis feels secondary or even self-protective. The person keeps moving, partly because movement sustains the identity that has become attached to continuation.

Across these settings, no single incident creates the moral charge. It accumulates through praise, dependence, memory, and repeated demonstrations of reliability. Once accumulated, it influences perception before conscious reasoning begins. A pause looks suspicious before its practical merits are considered. Continuation looks right before its current effectiveness is assessed. The sequence matters: interpretation precedes evaluation. Evaluation then confirms interpretation because the evaluative space has already been narrowed by moral significance.

This narrowing does not eliminate agency, but it alters its texture. Choices remain available, yet some choices feel preloaded with meaning. People continue not only to preserve outcomes, but to preserve legibility within a social field that has learned to read continuity as virtue. The field does not need to be hostile for this effect to occur. It only needs stable stories about what good people do under strain, and enough repetition for those stories to attach to specific individuals.

Weeks pass with ordinary tasks and ordinary conversations. The work gets done, messages get answered, and relational bonds remain intact. Beneath this routine, the unresolved question persists: is continuation being chosen for present conditions, or for coherence with a moral identity already in circulation? The question rarely produces immediate change. It remains open across days, then across seasons, while the same pattern repeats in slightly different forms and continuation keeps its ethical glow.

In that open state, judgment often remains partial. It notices the dignity in sustained commitment and the pressure embedded within that dignity. It sees how continuation can be both sincere and socially reinforced, both caring and constraining. No final verdict settles the tension. The chapter of activity continues with the same visible steadiness, while interpretation lags behind behavior and the moral meaning attached to continuation remains active in the background.

Moralization often intensifies when continuation is narrated publicly as an example. A person's persistence is cited in team meetings, shared in retrospectives, or referenced in informal mentoring conversations. The intent is appreciation, and appreciation is genuine. At the same time, exemplar status increases symbolic cost of deviation. Once someone is positioned as proof of a value, ordinary reconsideration can appear like contradiction of that value, even when practical conditions have changed.

In community settings, the same mechanism can develop around invisible service roles. One member handles recurring coordination over years and becomes associated with commitment itself. New participants inherit this interpretation without seeing the full history. They assume continuity is both natural and ethical. The role-holder may continue willingly and still feel a narrowing of legitimate options. The narrowing is social before it is procedural, but its practical effects are real.

Temporal delay makes this difficult to detect. No single moment converts practical continuation into moral expectation. The conversion happens through dozens of small affirmations, each reasonable in isolation. Later, when the person contemplates pausing, they face a dense field of prior affirmations that now function like obligations.

The field is not hostile. It is coherent, and coherence can itself exert pressure.

Another repeated scene appears in internal self-talk after ordinary setbacks. Instead of asking whether the current structure fits present conditions, the person evaluates whether continued effort aligns with the identity already established. Identity-focused evaluation tends to yield the same result: maintain continuity, preserve legibility, postpone structural questioning. The result is not guaranteed, but it is common when moral framing has become dominant.

Across contexts, continuation keeps receiving ethical interpretation while structural interpretation remains secondary. This does not invalidate continued commitment. It leaves unresolved whether commitment is being renewed for present realities or maintained to avoid symbolic discontinuity. The unresolved condition can persist for long periods without obvious external conflict.

Days continue normally: work progresses, relationships hold, responsibilities are met. Beneath that normality, moral meaning remains attached to repetition, and repetition keeps reinforcing moral meaning. The cycle stays active without producing a decisive break.

One more recurring situation appears during external recognition moments. An award, compliment, or public thank-you confirms the moral narrative around continuity. The recognition is sincere and often deserved. It also narrows interpretive space by linking identity to repetition once again. After recognition, ordinary hesitation can feel disloyal to the image just reinforced, even when practical conditions remain mixed.

This reinforcement does not resolve the underlying structural question. It postpones it. People keep carrying responsibilities with visible steadiness while privately sorting whether steadiness reflects current alignment or inherited moral expectation. The sorting remains incomplete, and continuation remains socially legible in the meantime.

This pattern can continue through long periods without explicit conflict. Continuation remains understandable, observers remain supportive, and moral framing remains available as a stable explanation for staying engaged. Structural ambiguity, meanwhile, remains largely in the background.

As a result, the person may keep participating with full visible commitment while still carrying unresolved evaluation about why participation continues and what meaning is being preserved by that continuity.

Across these continued cycles, no final judgment is required for the pattern to persist. Continuation remains visible and valued, while interpretation of that continuation remains partially unsettled. The person can remain sincere, reliable, and careful, and still carry unresolved tension between structural fit and moral legibility.

This unresolved state can continue through routine weeks where nothing forces explicit reconsideration. Work is completed, roles are maintained, and social meaning around persistence remains intact. The person keeps moving within that meaning while structural evaluation remains partially deferred.

Chapter 6

When Past Effort Starts to Speak for the Future

At some point, the reason for continuing is no longer located in the present.

It shifts quietly into the past.

People begin to reference what has already been done. Time invested. Energy spent. Reputation built. Relationships maintained.

These references feel reasonable. They ground decisions. They prevent waste.

But they also change how judgment operates.

When past effort begins to speak for the future, evaluation subtly reverses direction. Instead of asking what the situation now requires, the question becomes how to honor what has already been given.

This reversal is easy to miss because it does not feel irrational. Respecting prior effort feels responsible.

Early on, past effort is simply context. It informs understanding. It explains how things arrived here.

Later, it becomes justification.

Continuation is framed as protection of investment. Stopping is framed as loss.

This framing carries emotional weight. Loss feels heavier than stagnation. Waste feels worse than fatigue.

As a result, the future is evaluated through the lens of preservation. Options are weighed by what they would invalidate, not by what they would enable.

This is not a conscious calculation. It emerges through repetition.

Each day of continuation adds to the past. Each added layer increases the pressure to justify it. The longer something has been sustained, the harder it becomes to question.

Importantly, this pressure does not depend on success. Even uncertain or mediocre outcomes can generate strong attachment.

What matters is not quality, but accumulation.

Accumulation creates narrative. A story of effort. A story of endurance. A story of identity.

Once a narrative exists, future actions are expected to align with it.

Stopping threatens coherence. It introduces a break in the story. It raises uncomfortable questions.

Was the effort misguided? Was the investment misjudged? Was the commitment misplaced?

These questions are rarely welcomed. They imply error, and error challenges self-image.

Continuation avoids this challenge. It allows the story to remain intact. It reframes difficulty as perseverance.

This reframing is socially reinforced. Persistence is admired. Quitting is suspect. Consistency is praised.

Even when no one explicitly demands continuation, the cultural backdrop supplies pressure.

The past becomes heavier because it is visible.

Others have seen the effort. They recognize the role. They expect continuity.

These expectations may be vague, but they are felt.

Over time, people internalize them. They begin to speak to themselves using the language of obligation.

"I have already put so much into this." "It would be wrong to stop now." "I owe it to what I've built."

This language feels grounded, but it quietly displaces present judgment.

The current situation becomes secondary. Signals of misalignment are reinterpreted as temporary setbacks.

Discomfort is normalized. Doubt is postponed.

The future becomes a continuation of the past rather than an open field of evaluation.

This is why people often feel stuck without feeling trapped.

Nothing external is preventing exit. The constraint is internal, but it is structured, not emotional.

The past has been given authority.

This authority is difficult to challenge because it appears reasonable. After all, effort should count for something.

The problem is not that effort matters. The problem is that it begins to matter more than present conditions.

When this happens, judgment loses immediacy. It defers to history.

History becomes a proxy for legitimacy.

Understanding this does not require rejecting commitment. It does not imply that past effort was mistaken. It does not demand reversal.

It simply reveals how time can harden into constraint when effort is allowed to justify itself.

Past effort cannot decide the future. It can inform it. It can contextualize it.

But when it speaks in place of judgment, continuation stops being chosen and starts being inherited.

A common scene begins with a spreadsheet of prior investment. Hours are logged, milestones are archived, and each phase has a documented sequence of effort that seems too substantial to ignore. During review meetings, current conditions are discussed briefly, then conversation returns to what has already been spent. The archive exerts gravity. Participants speak as though the recorded past contains an implicit commitment about what must come next. Nobody states that history should decide, yet history repeatedly sets the boundary of what appears acceptable.

In early stages, references to past effort provide orientation. They help people remember why a project exists and what assumptions shaped its design. Later, the same references begin functioning as obligation. Language shifts from context to debt: "after everything invested," "given how far we've come," "considering all the work behind this." These phrases are understandable, but they quietly move authority from present signals to accumulated input. The future is approached less as open evaluation and more as continuation of what has already been justified.

The same pattern appears in personal commitments that evolve over years. A person stays in a demanding arrangement partly because leaving now would reframe earlier sacrifices. Memories of effort do not remain descriptive; they become active arguments. The individual can list current misalignments clearly, yet those misalignments are weighed against a narrative of endurance that has grown dense over time. The narrative does not prove that continuation is right. It does make alternatives feel like repudiations of the past.

Hesitation before judgment intensifies when the past includes public visibility. Others have witnessed the effort, praised persistence, and incorporated it into expectations. A change in direction would not occur in private; it would revise a shared story. Anticipating that revision introduces friction even before any decision is made. People delay judgment, reopen old calculations, and search for a way to preserve narrative continuity while still acknowledging present conditions. The search can continue for long periods without producing a stable conclusion.

Institutional projects often show this dynamic in budget cycles. Initial funding is justified by forecast, and subsequent funding is justified by prior funding. The logic becomes recursive. If so much has already been allocated, stopping seems to convert expenditure into acknowledged loss. Continuing keeps the possibility of eventual return alive, even when leading indicators remain ambiguous. This does not require denial of reality. It requires only that accumulated cost be treated as a claim on future action rather than as historical fact.

Temporal delay plays a central role. In the moment, each additional commitment looks small compared with the total already invested. Because increments are small, they appear easy to approve. Months later, the aggregate shift is substantial, and observers struggle to identify when exactly the threshold was crossed. No dramatic event marks the transition. Past effort gradually becomes the primary speaker in decisions that nominally concern the future. By the time this is visible, a new layer of investment has already been added.

A repeated structure appears across contexts: a present concern is raised, someone references prior effort, tension declines, and continuation proceeds. The concern is not dismissed outright; it is absorbed by the weight of history. This absorption feels rational in the room because prior effort is real and emotionally legible. Current uncertainty is less legible. The asymmetry favors continuation even when present evidence does not strengthen. The meeting ends with temporary relief and no clear increase in directional confidence.

In research settings, years of data collection can create similar pressure. Investigators remain attached to a line of inquiry partly because exiting would leave large datasets without the hoped-for narrative arc. The data still have value, but the value is experienced through the lens of intended destination. Deviating from that destination feels like violating the implied promise made by earlier labor. Discussion returns to what has already been built, not because alternatives are impossible, but because alternatives would reinterpret the meaning of accumulated work.

Personal finance decisions can show the same geometry. Someone continues supporting an underperforming venture because stopping would force a reclassification of past contributions. Contributions were made in good faith and often under difficult conditions. Reclassifying them as irrecoverable feels harsher than continuing with uncertain prospects. The person is not unaware of current limitations. They are navigating a frame where past effort carries emotional authority. That authority complicates present judgment and stretches the period of indecision.

The social layer reinforces everything. Narratives of perseverance are widely admired, while narratives of revision can be misunderstood as inconsistency. People absorb these norms and apply
them to themselves. They continue partly to remain legible within
a culture that treats endurance as evidence of character. Present
conditions remain visible but secondary. Historical commitment
appears as the more stable indicator of legitimacy. Legitimacy then
guides choice, sometimes more strongly than contemporaneous fit.

Across long time horizons, history can become mistaken for
forecast. Because effort persisted for years, continuation feels sta-
tistically probable and therefore justified. Yet probability of continuation is not probability of improved fit. This distinction is often
recognized abstractly but not operationally. Day-to-day decisions
still reference accumulated investment as if it contains directional
information. The reference is understandable, and it can coexist with
thoughtful analysis. Still, its repeated presence tilts judgment toward
inherited momentum.

The internal experience is often one of divided clarity. On one
side, there is a calm recognition that present indicators are mixed or
stagnant. On the other side, there is a heavy sense that prior sacrifice
must not be rendered meaningless. The two perceptions are not
mutually exclusive, which is why resolution comes slowly. People
continue to act while carrying both frames at once. Action sustains
the past-facing frame because each new action becomes additional
history that must later be honored.

Another scene repeats in quiet moments: old notebooks, archived
plans, and early correspondence are revisited. Reading them evokes

seriousness, optimism, and effort that was unquestionably real. The emotional impact of that record can re-legitimize continuation for another interval, even when current conditions remain unchanged. The record does not dictate a decision, but it alters the perceived cost of divergence. Divergence now appears to challenge not only current plans but the dignity of earlier work.

In group settings, no one person needs to advocate strongly for continuation. The structure can carry itself. One member references sunk time, another mentions reputational exposure, another notes stakeholder expectations, and the combined effect restores forward motion. Present doubts are acknowledged, then deferred. Minutes are recorded, actions assigned, and the next checkpoint is scheduled. Between checkpoints, additional effort is invested, which increases the historical weight available at the next discussion.

This loop can persist without overt conflict. Participants may be thoughtful, transparent, and aware of tradeoffs. What maintains the loop is not confusion alone; it is the authority granted to prior effort in moments that demand present judgment. The authority feels earned. It is earned as memory. Whether it should function as mandate remains unresolved. That unresolved status allows continuation to appear both rational and heavy at the same time.

Weeks and quarters pass with ordinary work and ordinary language. The future is discussed, yet arguments repeatedly route through the past. No final decision arrives to settle the relationship between history and current fit. Instead, continuation proceeds through incremental endorsements. Each endorsement adds new effort to the archive, and the archive continues speaking with a voice that sounds increasingly difficult to challenge.

The scene remains open: people continue meeting, records continue growing, and present conditions continue being interpreted through what has already been given. The process does not collapse into certainty. It extends, measured in additional cycles where the past remains near the center of decisions that are formally about what comes next.

Past effort can also speak through artifacts that make continuation feel already decided. Roadmaps, public commitments, and archived presentations remain visible long after conditions shift. These artifacts were created under earlier assumptions, yet they continue shaping conversation because they are concrete and shareable. Present uncertainty, by contrast, is harder to package. In meetings, concrete history can outweigh less concrete current signals, and continuation proceeds with minimal explicit debate.

In grant-funded or donor-supported work, prior investment carries additional reputational weight. People worry that directional change will be interpreted as misuse of trust, even when change is a reasonable response to new information. To avoid this interpretation, teams often continue along inherited lines while reframing adjustments as minor refinements. The reframing preserves narrative continuity and delays direct evaluation of whether the inherited line still fits present conditions.

Another repeated scene is personal and archival: someone re-opens early plans, sees the seriousness of original commitments, and feels renewed obligation to honor that seriousness through continued effort. The renewed obligation may coexist with current doubt. Neither fully cancels the other. Action tends to follow obligation in the short term because obligation is clearer than doubt and easier to explain publicly.

Over longer periods, this pattern converts history into a default decision mechanism. No explicit rule states that past effort should dominate, yet choices repeatedly align with that outcome. The present is consulted, but the past remains the stronger voice. The imbalance may be recognized and still persist because reversing it would require reinterpretation of accumulated work, and reinterpretation is socially and psychologically costly.

The process remains open. New effort is added, the archive grows, and each additional layer increases the amount of history available to justify subsequent continuation. Present judgment remains active but partially deferred to what has already been done.

The same tension appears when external stakeholders ask for updates. Teams present continuity because continuity is easiest to communicate, and continuity then reinforces the authority of prior effort. Present doubts are translated into cautious wording rather than directional reconsideration. The meeting ends with adjusted timelines and unchanged trajectory.

History therefore keeps participating in decisions as an active force, not only as a record. It remains useful as context and heavy as mandate, while present evaluation continues alongside it without fully displacing it.

Where this continues, future planning sessions often sound decisive while remaining historically anchored. Plans are updated, language is refreshed, and execution resumes, yet the underlying authority of prior effort remains largely intact. Present evidence participates, but it does not fully govern.

The result is ongoing motion under inherited direction, with evaluation repeatedly filtered through what has already been invested.

So the future continues to be negotiated in conversation with the past, with neither fully overriding the other. Historical investment remains influential, present signals remain active, and continuation proceeds while their relative authority stays unresolved.

As that negotiation continues, present judgment and historical obligation remain entangled. Decisions still get made, timelines still move, and effort still accumulates, while the question of which signal should lead remains open across successive cycles.

Chapter 7

Why Stopping Feels Like Losing Structure

For many people, the idea of stopping does not feel neutral.

It does not feel like choosing differently. It feels like removing something that holds things together.

This reaction is often surprising. Nothing obvious suggests collapse. No rule states that stopping will cause harm.

Yet the sensation persists. Stopping feels destabilizing.

This feeling does not come from danger. It comes from structure.

Over time, continuation does more than maintain activity. It organizes time, attention, and identity.

Schedules align around it. Expectations adapt to it. Self-understanding incorporates it.

Continuation becomes a reference point.

When that reference point is threatened, the surrounding structure becomes uncertain. Not because it cannot exist without it, but because it has not been imagined without it.

Most people underestimate how much structure their ongoing commitments quietly provide.

They create rhythm. They define priorities. They offer justification for effort.

Even difficulty gains meaning through continuity. Strain is tolerable when it fits a pattern.

Stopping interrupts this pattern.

Without continuation, questions emerge that were previously answered implicitly.

What fills the time? What justifies the effort? What defines the role?

These questions are not abstract. They are practical and immediate.

Stopping creates a gap. That gap demands orientation.

Orientation requires energy. It requires reflection. It requires tolerating ambiguity.

Continuation avoids this cost. It preserves orientation without reexamination.

This is why stopping often feels harder than continuing, even when continuation is exhausting.

Exhaustion occurs within a known structure. Stopping requires forming a new one.

The fear here is not inactivity. It is unstructured activity.

Many people are comfortable being busy. They are less comfortable being undefined.

Continuation supplies definition. It answers "what am I doing" without deliberation.

When continuation has been sustained for long enough, this definition becomes implicit. It no longer feels like a choice.

Stopping threatens to expose the absence of an alternative structure.

This exposure feels like loss, even if nothing tangible is taken away.

The loss is of coherence.

Coherence allows effort to feel justified. It connects actions to identity. It supports endurance.

When coherence is disrupted, even temporarily, people experience discomfort.

They describe it as restlessness, unease, or anxiety.

These sensations are often misattributed. People assume they are symptoms of laziness, lack of discipline, or insufficient motivation.

In reality, they are responses to structural ambiguity.

Stopping removes a scaffold. The building does not collapse, but it sways.

This sway is tolerable, but it is unfamiliar. Unfamiliar sensations are often interpreted as warning signs.

Continuation returns stability. The sway stops. The system feels firm again.

This reinforces the belief that continuation is necessary for stability.

Over time, the association strengthens. Stopping equals disorder. Continuing equals control.

This binary is false, but it is compelling.

The truth is more subtle. Continuation supplies structure, but it is not the only possible structure.

However, forming alternative structures requires time and imagination. It cannot be done instantly.

Because stopping is often imagined as immediate and absolute, its transitional nature is overlooked.

People imagine chaos where there would be adjustment.

This imagination magnifies perceived risk.

It becomes easier to continue than to confront the unknown shape of what comes next.

Importantly, this does not mean stopping is desirable. It means stopping is underdefined.

Continuation is familiar. Stopping is vague.

Familiarity feels safe. Vagueness feels risky.

As long as stopping remains vague, it will feel disproportionate.

Understanding this does not instruct anyone to stop. It does not minimize the real costs of transition.

It simply explains why stopping feels heavier than continuing, even when continuation is draining.

The weight is not danger. It is the absence of ready-made structure.

Once this absence is recognized, stopping can be evaluated more clearly, not as collapse, but as reorientation.

Until then, continuation feels like the only way to keep things together.

From an observer viewpoint, the sense that stopping equals disorder often appears in environments where continuity has become an organizing scaffold rather than a simple habit. Workflows, calendars, and shared assumptions are arranged around an ongoing line of activity, so interruption is experienced first as structural ambiguity. The individual may describe this as personal anxiety, yet at system level it resembles a temporary loss of reference coordinates. Other actors in the same environment can feel it too, even when no one announces it directly.

In organizations, this shows up when a long-running process is paused and participants immediately ask coordination questions that were previously automatic. Who owns the next step, what timing replaces the old rhythm, where does pending effort now belong. None of these questions indicates failure. They indicate that a structure once supplied by continuation is now visible as structure because it is missing. The same sequence repeats in families, teams, and community groups: coherence was present, but mostly unnoticed until the reference pattern softened.

Recognition is often delayed because continuation makes itself appear natural. People interpret recurring schedules and role clarity as given facts rather than maintained arrangements. Only later, sometimes after several discontinuous periods, do they notice how much orientation had been borrowed from repetition. What looked like personal reluctance to stop can then be reframed as a predictable reaction to temporary underdefinition. This reframing usually arrives after the most intense uncertainty has already passed.

At greater distance, the pattern has little drama. Systems move from defined rhythm to underdefined interval, then toward a different rhythm. During the underdefined interval, ordinary tasks still occur, but prioritization becomes noisier and interpretive load increases. Participants spend more energy establishing local meaning for small actions because shared scaffolding is thinner. The discomfort is real, though often short-lived. It does not necessarily point to danger; it points to reorganization costs distributed across daily interactions.

Quiet repetition reinforces the point over time. Whenever continuation is restored, immediate relief is interpreted as proof that restoration was necessary. Whenever continuation is interrupted, temporary ambiguity is interpreted as warning. Both interpretations are understandable and both can be misleading when viewed in isolation. Across many cycles, the broader observation remains steady: structure and familiarity are being conflated, and the felt risk of stopping is partly the felt effort of redefining structure in public time.

Seen from this angle, the chapter remains in a suspended state where continuation keeps providing ready-made coherence and stopping keeps appearing larger than it is because its transitional phase is repeatedly encountered at close range and remembered as threat. The environment continues operating, roles continue adapting, and the structural question stays active without requiring immediate resolution.

Another observer-level pattern appears when people try brief interruptions after long continuity. During the interruption, most functions continue, but local confusion rises around sequencing and ownership. Participants experience this confusion at close range and often overestimate its long-term significance. Later analysis frequently shows that confusion was transitional and self-correcting. Yet what is remembered most clearly is the immediate disorientation, not the gradual reorganization that followed. Memory then reinforces the view that stopping is inherently destabilizing.

In networked teams, structure is also carried by informal routines that are rarely documented. A person who has continued for years becomes a routing point for decisions, clarifications, and emotional calibration. When continuation pauses, formal charts still exist, but informal routing thins. The group describes this as losing momentum, though part of what is lost is simply an implicit map that had been maintained through repetition. Over time, groups often rebuild a map, but the rebuilding period can be interpreted as evidence that continuation was the only workable option.

Time-delayed recognition tends to occur after several cycles of pause and restart. People begin to notice that each pause produced similar early ambiguity followed by gradual pattern formation. The early ambiguity had looked exceptional in the moment, but later appears recurrent and predictable. This changes the interpretation of instability from permanent threat to transitional cost. The reinterpretation usually arrives slowly, because it requires comparing multiple intervals rather than reacting to one.

At structural distance, stopping is less a binary event and more a reallocation problem. Rhythms, responsibilities, and self-descriptions that were synchronized by continuation need temporary re-synchronization through other cues. The cost is real: more explicit communication, more provisional roles, more local uncertainty. The cost is also bounded. Systems that continue interacting usually generate replacement structures over time, even when participants initially experience the interval as diffuse and uncomfortable.

The quiet repetition remains consistent across contexts: continuation supplies low-friction order, interruption reveals underdocumented dependencies, and participants interpret the revealing moment as danger because it is immediate and vivid. Across longer timelines, many of those same participants observe that structure did not vanish; it changed form at a pace that was harder to notice while living inside it.

Observer accounts also show how role memory reinforces this pattern. Even after continuity loosens, surrounding actors continue addressing a person through the previous structure, asking for the same pacing and the same type of immediate orientation. The person experiences this as pressure to restore order quickly. Others experience it as normal coordination. The same interaction is interpreted differently depending on distance from the underlying reorganization.

Over time, repeated returns to old role expectations can make transition look like repeated failure to stabilize, when it is partly repeated social recall of older maps. Groups continue functioning through this phase, but with a persistent tendency to treat temporary underdefinition as evidence that only the previous structure can work.

Across multiple cycles, the pattern stays quiet and familiar: continuity provides instant legibility, interruption reveals hidden scaffolding, and legibility is mistaken for necessity because it is encountered as immediate relief.

From a cross-context perspective, this structural feeling of loss also persists because people rarely pause long enough to observe the full transition curve from old coherence to interim ambiguity to new coherence. Most experience only fragments: the first days of disorientation, a period of redistributed effort, then a return to familiar demands under a slightly altered map. Because attention is highest during the disorientation fragment, that fragment dominates interpretation and is later recalled as proof that stopping threatens system integrity. In practice, many systems continue functioning during transition with mixed efficiency rather than collapse. Tasks still move, but ownership becomes more explicit; communication still occurs, but with less shorthand; priorities still exist, but with less automatic ranking. These changes require effort that continuation had previously hidden. The effort is often read as danger because it is visible and immediate. Over successive cycles, organizations and households can become caught in a subtle loop where they repeatedly avoid transitional effort, then cite absence of transition experience as evidence that alternatives to continuation are unreal or unsafe. This loop has no single author and no dramatic turning point. It is maintained by ordinary memory, ordinary planning pressure, and ordinary preference for already-legible structures. Observers mapping several years of activity often note that the system's capacity to reorganize was never absent; it was simply underexercised and therefore repeatedly interpreted as unavailable.

When viewed after several such intervals, the same people often report that what felt like structural loss in one moment was partly a temporary loss of familiar sequencing cues. Tasks still had possible paths, but those paths required explicit negotiation instead of inherited momentum. As soon as explicit negotiation started recurring, a new rhythm appeared and again became ordinary.

With repeated exposure, participants often begin distinguishing temporary ambiguity from structural breakdown, but this distinction usually emerges only after several transitions have already been experienced as threat.

The same cycle then repeats in quieter form, with continuity repeatedly preferred because it is instantly legible, while transitional legibility remains delayed and therefore repeatedly underrated.

That preference continues to reproduce itself through ordinary scheduling, ordinary memory, and ordinary avoidance of transitional ambiguity.

The pattern remains in place across routine cycles.

Chapter 8

When Continuation Feels Like the Only Stable Option

There is a point where continuation no longer feels like a preference. It feels like the only position that keeps things from wobbling.

This sensation does not come from certainty. It comes from contrast.

Everything else feels undefined.

When stopping is imagined as disorientation, continuation inherits the role of stability. Not because it is optimal, but because it is familiar.

Familiarity is powerful. It reduces cognitive load. It answers questions before they are asked.

What am I doing? Why am I doing it? What happens next?

Continuation supplies ready-made answers. They may not be satisfying, but they are available.

In contrast, alternatives require construction. They need to be articulated, tested, adjusted.

This construction takes time. It demands patience with ambiguity.

Most people do not avoid alternatives because they are lazy. They avoid them because ambiguity is expensive.

Ambiguity consumes attention. It destabilizes routine. It interrupts momentum.

Continuation avoids this cost. It keeps the machinery running.

Over time, the relief provided by continuation is misinterpreted as proof of correctness.

The system feels calmer when you stay. Tension reduces. Questions quiet down.

This calmness is real, but it is not evidence of alignment. It is evidence of reduced friction.

Friction emerges when assumptions are challenged. Continuation leaves assumptions intact.

As long as the system remains unchallenged, it feels smooth.

This smoothness becomes addictive. Not emotionally, but structurally.

People begin to associate discomfort with danger, and comfort with safety.

Stopping threatens comfort, so it is framed as unsafe.

This framing does not require conscious belief. It operates through sensation.

Imagining continuation feels steady. Imagining stopping feels jittery.

The body reacts before the mind evaluates.

Because of this, people often say they "feel" that continuing is right. The feeling is genuine. The interpretation is questionable.

The feeling reflects stability, not direction.

Stability can exist without progress. It can exist without meaning. It can exist simply because nothing is being disturbed.

This is why systems can feel stable long after they have stopped moving forward.

Continuation preserves equilibrium. Equilibrium feels good.

But equilibrium is not the same as health.

A system can be stable because it is balanced, or because opposing forces cancel each other out.

From the inside, both feel similar.

This similarity makes evaluation difficult. People sense calm and assume correctness.

When alternatives are vague, their imagined costs loom larger than their benefits. Continuation, by comparison, feels safe.

This asymmetry biases judgment.

Options are not weighed evenly. One option feels solid. The others feel hypothetical.

Hypotheticals are easy to dismiss. They have no weight yet.

Continuation has weight because it already exists.

This weight grows over time. The longer something is sustained, the more effort has been invested in it. The more effort invested, the more reality it acquires.

Reality feels safer than possibility.

This is how continuation becomes the default. Not through argument, but through inertia.

Inertia is not resistance to change. It is the absence of force pushing in another direction.

Stopping requires force. It requires intention. It requires accepting a period of imbalance.

Continuation requires none of these. It simply continues.

This asymmetry explains why people remain in situations they cannot fully justify.

They are not convinced. They are stabilized.

Stabilization is often mistaken for conviction.

Others may reinforce this mistake. They observe consistency and infer confidence. They see persistence and assume purpose.

These interpretations feed back into the system. They increase the perceived cost of deviation.

If everyone else sees stability, stopping begins to look disruptive.

Disruption attracts attention. Attention invites explanation. Explanation demands clarity.

When clarity is incomplete, continuation feels safer.

This safety is relative. It is safety from scrutiny, not safety from cost.

Costs still exist. They accumulate quietly. They are spread over time.

Because they do not spike, they are tolerated.

Stopping concentrates cost. It produces immediate friction. Continuation distributes it.

Distributed cost is easier to bear, even if the total is larger.

This is another reason continuation feels reasonable. It smooths pain rather than eliminating it.

Understanding this does not transform continuation into a mistake. It reveals why it persists without endorsement.

Continuation feels like the only stable option because stability has been narrowly defined.

Stability is equated with non-disruption. With maintaining shape. With preserving rhythm.

Other forms of stability exist, but they require transition. Transition feels unstable by definition.

As long as transition is avoided, continuation will dominate judgment.

Not because it is best, but because it is already there.

Recognizing this does not force a decision. It simply restores proportion.

Continuation is stable, but it is not uniquely so.

It is one way to avoid immediate imbalance, not the only way to sustain oneself over time.

When this distinction becomes visible, continuation loses its monopoly on safety.

It becomes an option again, not a necessity.

A frequent scene begins at the start of a week when plans are reviewed and alternatives are briefly acknowledged. Several options exist in theory: reduce scope, change timelines, redistribute responsibility, or pause certain activities. Each option requires explanation, negotiation, and temporary disorganization. Continuation requires none of that immediate construction. The current arrangement is already loaded into calendars, habits, and expectations. By midday, discussion shifts from alternatives to execution, not because alternatives were disproven, but because continuation offered the shortest path to recognizable order.

This sequence repeats in many domains. In a company, a team keeps an inefficient process because everyone knows its sequence and failure modes. Replacing it might eventually improve outcomes, but replacement demands a period where people are uncertain about roles and timing. In a household, routines continue even when they feel cramped because redesigning them would require multiple conversations with unclear results. In personal work, familiar patterns persist because unfamiliar patterns have no tested structure yet. Stability is experienced as familiarity in motion.

Hesitation before judgment often centers on ambiguity costs. People can tolerate known strain more easily than undefined transition. Known strain has predictable contours: busy hours, recurring tension points, manageable fatigue. Undefined transition has unknown contours: temporary confusion, social interpretation, possible missteps without clear blame. When these two are compared, continuation appears prudent because its costs are distributed and familiar. The comparison may be incomplete, but it feels concrete, and concreteness tends to dominate in daily decisions.

In meetings, this appears as preference for options with immediate clarity rather than long-term coherence. A plan that preserves existing rhythms receives faster agreement. A plan that introduces short-term uncertainty receives requests for further detail, then deferral. Deferral is not rejection. It is postponement in favor of what is already operational. Weeks pass, and the operational default becomes more deeply embedded. Later, the postponed alternative looks riskier partly because more commitments now depend on the unchanged arrangement.

The body also participates in this logic. Imagining continuation can produce a sense of steadiness because the sequence of next actions is known. Imagining deviation can produce physiological noise: faster thoughts, unsettled attention, fragmented focus. People may interpret these sensations as evidence that continuation is correct and alternatives are unsafe. The sensations are real. Their meaning remains ambiguous. They may indicate exposure to uncertainty rather than actual threat. In day-to-day life, that distinction is rarely investigated in depth.

A repeated pattern appears in communication behavior. Continuation allows familiar scripts: routine updates, standard responses, expected check-ins. Alternatives require new language, and new language risks misunderstanding. Because misunderstanding feels costly, people keep using established scripts. Scripts reinforce continuity by making each day easier to execute. The result is a self-reinforcing loop where linguistic ease supports structural inertia, and structural inertia further reduces appetite for linguistic change.

Temporal delay strengthens this loop. Each day of continuation is small and manageable, so it rarely triggers urgent reevaluation. Over months, however, the cumulative effect is large: assumptions harden, dependencies multiply, and imagination narrows to what the current structure can accommodate. By the time discomfort becomes undeniable, the unchanged system feels like the only stable option precisely because so much has been organized around it. Stability has been produced by repetition, not by explicit endorsement of underlying fit.

In educational settings, students and instructors can share this pattern. A course design with known limitations continues semester after semester because revisions would require coordination across departments and uncertain student response. Everyone can list the design's weaknesses, yet continuation remains easier to administer. The system feels stable because people have adapted their expectations to it. Adaptation is practical and often necessary. It can also mask how much effort is spent preserving a form that no longer serves its original intent efficiently.

In personal relationships, continuation can feel stable when roles are longstanding and predictable. Two people may keep a conversational pattern that leaves important issues untouched because altering the pattern could create temporary volatility. Everyday interactions remain functional, and that functionality is interpreted as stability. The unspoken material does not vanish; it remains outside routine exchange. The relationship does not collapse, and nothing visibly changes. Stability is maintained through repeated avoidance of uncertain transitions.

Another recurring scene occurs during short breaks. Someone steps away for a day or two and returns to find the same structure waiting, with accumulated tasks arranged in familiar order. Re-entry is straightforward. This ease reinforces continuation. It suggests that the existing system is resilient and dependable. A deeper look might show that resilience comes from the person's ability to resume compensation quickly. Because compensation is swift, structural questions are delayed again, and the cycle of stable continuation restarts.

Across these contexts, alternatives are not absent. They remain conceptual, partial, and underdeveloped. Continuation is fully developed because it is already being enacted. This asymmetry shapes judgment before formal analysis begins. The fully developed option appears safer because it has procedures, language, and social recognition. The conceptual option appears risky because it lacks these supports. Over time, this difference in developmental maturity is mistaken for difference in intrinsic validity.

Social interpretation also matters. Consistent continuation is easy for others to read as confidence. Any visible deviation can attract curiosity, concern, or criticism. Anticipating that attention adds cost to transition. People often choose continuation to avoid becoming a focal point of interpretation. The choice may be temporary, but temporary choices accumulate. What begins as a short-term preference for low visibility can become a long-term pattern where continuity is preserved primarily because it avoids social friction.

The internal narrative during this phase can remain ambivalent. A person may acknowledge that continuation is not ideal while still experiencing it as the only stable option available today. Tomorrow is expected to offer better conditions for reevaluation. Tomorrow arrives with similar constraints and similar incentives. Reevaluation is postponed again. This postponement is not necessarily denial; it is often an adaptive response to limited bandwidth. Adaptation keeps the system running and delays structural experimentation.

In organizations undergoing rapid change, continuation can paradoxically feel most stable when everything else is moving. Amid shifting priorities and uncertain leadership signals, maintaining one known routine offers an anchor. Teams cling to familiar workflows as a way to preserve local coherence. The anchor may not improve outcomes, but it reduces immediate cognitive strain. Reduced strain is experienced as safety, and safety is taken as evidence that the anchored routine should remain untouched.

Scene after scene returns to the same geometry: uncertainty is anticipated, continuation is selected, short-term friction decreases, and the selection is validated by temporary calm. Calm then becomes part of the argument for continuing. No final resolution appears. The system stays legible and therefore durable. People keep operating within it while recognizing, at least intermittently, that stability has been defined narrowly as non-disruption rather than as broader alignment.

The sequence remains open across time. Weekly planning cycles continue, routines remain in place, and alternatives remain possible but underconstructed. Continuation keeps its status as the only stable option, not because competing options are impossible, but because competing options have not yet been given enough form to compete with what is already running.

Continuation as stability is often reinforced by tooling itself. Dashboards, templates, and approval paths are built around current workflows. Using them feels smooth because they encode established assumptions. Alternatives require either adapting tools or working around them, both of which introduce temporary inefficiency and visibility. Teams facing tight schedules usually choose encoded stability over unencoded possibility. The choice is practical in the moment and cumulative over time.

Another recurring scene appears during handoffs. Existing routines make handoffs predictable: everyone knows where information lives and how exceptions are handled. Proposed changes create uncertainty about ownership during transition. To avoid miscommunication risk, teams postpone change and keep the old routine.

Postponement is narrated as caution. Caution preserves reliability today and increases attachment to continuity tomorrow.

In personal systems, stable continuation can depend on rituals that reduce decision fatigue. The ritual may no longer produce meaningful progress, yet it provides immediate orientation each morning. Breaking it would require designing a new structure under uncertainty. Many people continue the old ritual while acknowledging its limits because recognizable sequence can feel safer than experimental space.

These repetitions produce a durable impression that stability belongs to continuation alone. Other forms of stability remain theoretical because they are not yet enacted. As long as enactment is delayed, continuation keeps winning by default, and the system remains in familiar motion without a clear shift in direction.

During high-pressure periods, this preference for familiar stability strengthens further. People default to what can be executed immediately and postpone what must be invented under uncertainty. The postponement is practical, repeatable, and rarely controversial. It also keeps alternatives underdeveloped, which preserves the impression that continuation is the only workable form of stability.

As this repeats, stability and familiarity become nearly indistinguishable in everyday judgment. The system continues to run smoothly enough, and the distinction between running smoothly and moving meaningfully remains open.

So the system keeps selecting continuity in small, practical decisions that are easy to justify locally. Each local decision preserves short-term legibility and postpones broader redesign. Over time, those local decisions accumulate into a durable preference for the familiar, even when familiar no longer guarantees directional movement.

Within that pattern, continuity remains easier to enact than alternative stability, and ease keeps guiding choice. The system stays coherent in the short term while longer-term directional clarity remains pending.

So continuation remains the most immediately stable option in practice, even while alternatives remain conceptually available. The chapter stays in that practical asymmetry, where familiarity keeps winning small decisions and small decisions keep reinforcing familiarity.

Chapter 9

How Judgment Gets Quietly Displaced

Most people do not lose judgment all at once.

It is not taken away. It is not overridden. It is not replaced by force.

It becomes quieter.

The shift is subtle. Judgment is still present, but it no longer speaks first.

Other signals move ahead of it.

Urgency speaks. Habit speaks. Expectation speaks.

Judgment waits.

This waiting is rarely noticed. People assume judgment is working because they still think, still evaluate, still weigh options.

What has changed is timing.

Judgment no longer initiates. It responds.

By the time judgment is consulted, the direction is already leaning. Momentum has formed. Alternatives feel less available.

This displacement does not require suppression. It happens through crowding.

Continuation produces noise. Decisions need to be made. Responses are expected. Issues appear and disappear.

In this environment, judgment competes with immediacy.

Immediacy usually wins.

Not because it is wiser, but because it is louder.

The system rewards responsiveness. Quick replies reduce friction. Immediate action restores calm.

Each time immediacy resolves discomfort, it gains authority.

Judgment, by contrast, operates slowly. It requires distance. It asks for space.

Space is scarce when continuation is constant.

Over time, judgment adapts to scarcity. It shortens. It simplifies. It confines itself to local questions.

Instead of asking "Is this structure still aligned?" it asks "How do I handle this instance?"

This shift is efficient. It keeps things moving. It avoids disruption.

But it also narrows perspective.

Judgment becomes tactical. It optimizes within constraints it no longer examines.

Most people do not notice this narrowing. They remain thoughtful. They remain reflective.

What they lose is scope.

Scope is the ability to evaluate the frame, not just the contents.

Without scope, judgment cannot question continuation itself. It can only improve how continuation is executed.

This is why people often say "I've thought about it a lot" while feeling no closer to clarity.

They have thought deeply, but locally.

Their judgment has been busy, but contained.

Containment feels like responsibility. It appears mature. It avoids grand disruptions.

But it also prevents recalibration.

As judgment recedes, other criteria take precedence.

Consistency matters more than sense. Predictability matters more than fit. Stability matters more than meaning.

These priorities are rarely articulated. They are felt.

The system rewards them. Smoothness is praised. Disruption is discouraged.

Judgment learns to stay quiet because speaking up would introduce friction.

This quiet is not silence. It is self-restraint.

People learn which thoughts are useful and which are inconvenient. They bring forward what can be acted on and withhold what cannot.

Judgment becomes selective.

It does not disappear. It edits itself.

This editing is often unconscious. It feels like focus. It feels like discipline.

Over time, questions that cannot be answered immediately are deferred indefinitely.

Deferred questions fade. Not because they are resolved, but because they are rarely invited.

This is how judgment is displaced without being denied.

It remains present, but it no longer governs.

Understanding this does not require reclaiming judgment. It requires recognizing when it stopped leading.

The displacement is structural, not personal.

Anyone in a system that rewards continuity will experience it.

Judgment is not weak. It is outpaced.

When immediacy dominates, judgment adapts by shrinking.

Only when space returns does judgment regain its voice.

Until then, it waits quietly, aware, but unheard.

At system level, displacement of judgment is often visible as a timing shift rather than a belief shift. People continue to think carefully, but the sequence of events changes: response happens first, evaluation happens after response has already committed the direction. Over repeated cycles, this ordering becomes normal. External observers reviewing decisions over time can see that most choices were made under active momentum, with reflective framing added later as documentation or justification.

In high-velocity settings, this sequence is reinforced by coordination benefits. Fast replies keep communication smooth, reduce immediate uncertainty for others, and prevent escalation of minor tensions. Each short-term benefit is concrete and socially rewarded. Slower scope-level reflection has diffuse benefits that are harder to attribute to one moment. The result is not anti-judgment culture; it is a culture where judgment is compressed into narrow windows and asked to operate on already-moving structures.

Time-delayed recognition appears when participants look back and notice repetition: similar local optimizations recurring without broader frame revision. The same categories of issues are handled effectively each week, while the context that generates those issues remains largely unexamined. People often describe this later as being busy with important decisions while drifting on structural decisions. The description is less about error and more about sequencing under persistent demand.

From structural distance, the phenomenon has a neutral logic. Systems favor signals with immediate coordination value. Urgency and expectation are high-frequency signals; scope-level judgment is lower frequency and requires protected intervals. When protected intervals are repeatedly interrupted, judgment adapts by focusing on what can be processed quickly. This adaptation looks like discipline from inside daily work and like narrowing from outside longitudinal analysis.

Quiet repetition completes the pattern. Each day includes competent handling of immediate demands, each day leaves frame-level questions partially deferred, and each deferral slightly increases the density of future evaluation. No single day feels decisive. Across months, the cumulative effect is clear: judgment remains present, but its first-mover role has migrated to other signals that are louder, faster, and easier to coordinate around.

The chapter therefore stays in ongoing motion. Individuals continue acting responsibly within available constraints, systems continue rewarding immediacy, and recognition of displacement continues arriving later than the displacement itself.

A wider process view shows displacement through meeting architecture. Agendas are often organized around pending actions, blockers, and deadlines. This structure is practical and keeps coordination efficient. Over time, it can also reduce opportunities for frame-level judgment because questions about fit do not have a default slot. When such questions arise, they are deferred to separate sessions that are easier to postpone than action sessions. Participants continue making good local choices while broader evaluation windows shrink by scheduling logic alone.

Communication platforms contribute to the same effect. High-frequency channels reward short response times and immediate interpretability. Messages that ask for scope-level reflection are longer, slower, and more likely to be bypassed during active cycles. The channel does not prohibit judgment; it privileges signals that travel quickly. As teams adapt to channel tempo, judgment shifts toward what can be expressed and decided within that tempo. Scope narrows without explicit policy change.

Delayed recognition often appears in retrospective documents. Teams reviewing prior quarters see many well-executed interventions and still note recurring structural tensions. The recurrence does not imply poor execution. It suggests that execution has been operating ahead of recalibration. This observation is usually gentle rather than accusatory. People can see that everyone was responsive under real constraints while also seeing that responsiveness became the dominant allocator of attention.

From an external analytic standpoint, the pattern resembles temporal compression. Evaluation that once happened before commitment is moved into shorter windows after commitment. The system remains intelligent, but intelligence is concentrated on near-horizon stability. Distant-horizon coherence becomes periodic, then occasional. When distant-horizon sessions finally occur, they are asked to process large amounts of accumulated context in limited time, which further encourages partial deferral.

Quiet repetition then normalizes the arrangement. Each cycle starts with urgent items, each cycle ends with little space for frame review, and each cycle carries unresolved questions forward. Participants are aware enough to sense this movement, yet the daily advantages of immediacy keep the pattern intact. No single decision creates displacement. Repetition creates it.

Across longer periods, observers often note that the organization did not stop judging; it judged where time pressure allowed. The first-mover role simply migrated to faster signals embedded in routine coordination. Judgment remained present as a secondary pass, shaping interpretation after directional lean had already formed.

A further system-level view comes from how handoff culture evolves. When immediacy dominates, handoffs emphasize open items and urgent dependencies, while frame questions are described as context that can wait. Recipients inherit this ordering and continue it in the next cycle. The sequence becomes part of operational identity. People can work with high competence inside it and still find that frame-level judgment enters mostly at the margins.

Over long intervals, this creates a recognizable lag pattern. Structural concerns surface, get acknowledged, and are tagged for later windows that compete with fresh urgencies. Later windows arrive with larger backlogs of both action and interpretation. Participants narrow focus again to maintain flow. The lag deepens without requiring anyone to reject judgment in principle.

External reviewers often describe the result as a mature but compressed system: fast local adaptation, slower frame adaptation, high day-to-day responsiveness, and periodic difficulty changing underlying assumptions at the same pace. This description is neutral. It does not imply poor intent or weak thinking. It marks a stable timing arrangement produced by repeated operational choices.

A broader analytical frame also highlights how displacement of judgment can be reproduced through evaluation metrics that prioritize closure speed over frame quality. Teams are often measured on response latency, blocker removal, and throughput reliability, all of which are legitimate and useful indicators. Over time, these indicators can become the main grammar of competence. People then learn to make decisions that score well on immediate movement, while more complex frame checks are deferred because they do not map cleanly to the same dashboard cycle. This does not imply cynicism. Participants frequently care about frame quality and mention it explicitly in retrospectives. The issue is temporal mismatch: dashboards refresh daily or weekly, while frame revision may require comparative review across months. As a result, local success signals are continuously reinforced and scope-level concerns are episodically revisited under heavier cognitive load. Delayed recognition often appears when external auditors or internal strategy groups compare repeated quarters and notice that many local decisions were high quality while aggregate direction changed only minimally. The organization may be responsive at high frequency and conservative at low frequency without ever declaring that this is its model. Another quiet contributor is queue design. Items entering queues are usually concrete and actionable; frame questions are abstract and cross-cutting, so they are either translated into concrete items or left outside the queue. Translation can strip context. Exclusion can delay attention. Both outcomes narrow judgment's practical entry points. Over time, actors adapt by treating frame concerns as commentary around the work rather than part of the work sequence itself. This adaptation is efficient and cumulative. It produces a stable pattern in which judgment remains intellectually present yet operationally late, entering after enough directional momentum has built that alternatives feel expensive even before they are fully compared.

This timing structure can persist even in thoughtful teams because each immediate cycle presents legitimate reasons to preserve flow. By the time broader frame questions return, the operational context has shifted again, making direct comparison harder and narrowing the perceived room for alternatives. The result is a repeating delay in which judgment remains active but enters after coordination momentum has already reduced its effective range.

From outside, the pattern reads as sustained tactical intelligence coupled with delayed strategic voice, repeated until delay itself becomes part of the system's normal rhythm.

As this continues, judgment does not vanish; it continues to operate in constrained windows shaped by operational tempo, entering reliably but later than the signals that set direction first.

The lag remains structural, recurring whenever high-frequency coordination signals occupy most of the available attention budget.

This arrangement is sustained by routine coordination incentives, not by explicit rejection of broad judgment.

As this repeats, scope-level judgment remains present but routinely sequenced after high-frequency response demands.

Across repeated quarters, this sequencing pattern remains visible as a stable timing distribution: rapid local adjustment, deferred frame reassessment, and periodic recognition that strategic voice entered later than tactical voice. The sequence persists through ordinary operations and does not require explicit endorsement to continue.

Chapter 10

When Being Busy Replaces Deciding

As judgment recedes, activity often increases.

This increase feels responsible. It signals engagement. It creates the impression of control.

When questions become difficult, doing something feels better than waiting.

Busyness fills the space that judgment once occupied.

This substitution is rarely intentional. People do not decide to replace thinking with action. They respond to pressure.

Pressure demands response. Response produces motion. Motion produces relief.

That relief is immediate. Questions quiet down. Uncertainty recedes temporarily.

In this cycle, busyness begins to feel like decision-making.

Tasks are completed. Issues are addressed. Messages are answered.

From the outside, this looks like leadership. From the inside, it feels like coping.

Judgment requires pause. It needs time without demand. Busyness removes that time.

Each task interrupts reflection. Each interruption resets attention. The mind becomes reactive.

Reactivity is efficient. It keeps systems moving. It prevents accumulation.

But it also fragments awareness.

Judgment connects patterns. It looks across time. It notices direction.

Fragmented activity looks at the next item. It optimizes for immediacy. It values closure.

Closure feels satisfying. Completed tasks produce a sense of progress.

This sense is misleading. Progress is inferred from motion, not from alignment.

As long as things are being done, it feels like decisions are being made.

In reality, decisions are being avoided.

Busyness is attractive because it is measurable. Hours worked. Items checked off. Problems resolved.

Judgment is harder to measure. Its outcomes are delayed. Its value is ambiguous.

In environments that reward visibility, busyness becomes safer than deliberation.

People learn this quickly. They present activity as competence. They interpret stillness as risk.

This learning is reinforced socially. Those who respond fastest are seen as reliable. Those who hesitate are questioned.

Judgment hesitates by nature. It does not rush. It weighs.

When hesitation is penalized, judgment adapts by stepping aside.

Busyness steps forward.

Over time, people identify with their activity. They describe themselves as "busy" as if it explains everything.

Busyness becomes identity. It justifies exhaustion. It legitimizes strain.

When exhaustion appears, it is framed as workload, not misalignment.

The solution becomes efficiency. Better systems. Faster tools. More delegation.

These changes reduce friction, but they do not restore judgment.

They accelerate motion.

Acceleration increases dependency. The faster things move, the harder it becomes to stop.

Stopping would interrupt flow. Interruption feels costly.

Thus busyness sustains itself.

People feel trapped in activity while believing they are choosing.

They are choosing how to respond, not what to sustain.

This distinction matters.

Responding decides the next step. Judgment decides the direction.

When response dominates, direction drifts unnoticed.

Drift does not announce itself. It accumulates.

One task leads to another. One obligation generates the next. The structure perpetuates itself.

Because nothing breaks, the drift is tolerated.

People say they will think later. When things calm down. When time allows.

But calm rarely arrives on its own. Busyness prevents it.

This is not because people lack discipline. It is because activity has become the organizing principle.

Understanding this does not require abandoning effort. It requires seeing what effort is now doing.

Busyness feels like control because it reduces anxiety.

Judgment increases anxiety before it reduces it.

In environments that avoid discomfort, busyness will always win.

Until space is reclaimed, judgment remains secondary.

Not absent, but postponed.

Postponement can last a very long time.

Still busy.

Still moving.

Still responding.

Nothing breaks.

Nothing announces itself.

The next item.

Then the next.

A message answered.

A task completed.

A list shortened.

A list replaced.

Motion.

Relief.

Motion again.

Judgment waits.

Not absent.

Postponed.

Postponed again.

The day fills.

The space narrows.

Questions quiet down.

Not gone.

Quieted.

Busyness looks like certainty.

Busyness sounds like certainty.

Hours accumulate.

So do reasons.

So do obligations.

More done.

Less seen.

The system works.

The system costs.

Both can be true.

Both can stay unnamed.

One more response.

One more adjustment.

One more reassurance.

No clear moment.

No clear break.

Only continuation.

Continuation that feels responsible.

Continuation that feels necessary.

Continuation that feels automatic.

Direction stays quiet.

Activity stays loud.

Judgment does not disappear.

Judgment waits.

Waiting can look like delay.

Delay can look like risk.

So busyness steps in.

Again.

Again.

Again.

Nothing dramatic.

Nothing final.

Just the next task.

Just the next answer.

Just the next small completion.

A day like this.

Then another.

Then another.

Momentum without statement.

Momentum without question.

Momentum without pause.

Pause feels expensive.

So the pause is deferred.

Deferred into later.

Deferred into someday.

Deferred into after this cycle.

After this cycle becomes another cycle.

And another.

Judgment waits.

Still waiting.

In the background.

Close enough to feel.

Far enough to postpone.

The structure holds.

The structure tightens.

Nothing breaks.

Still nothing breaks.

The list moves.

The list returns.

The day ends.

The day restarts.

More motion.

More relief.

More motion.

Not resolution.

Not collapse.

Just continuation.

And continuation.

And continuation.

A quiet substitution.

A quiet exchange.

Activity where deciding used to be.

Not wrong.

Not right.

Just active.

Just measurable.

Just visible.

What is visible wins.

What is quiet waits.

Judgment waits.

Not absent.

Postponed.

Still postponed.

The system works.

The system costs.

Nothing breaks.

Not yet a conclusion.

Not yet a change.

Only space getting thinner.

Only pace getting faster.

Only questions returning between tasks.

Then the next task.

Then the next.

Then the next.

And the same quiet line underneath:

judgment waits.

One more cycle.

One more clear answer.

One more unopened question.

The ratio shifts quietly.

More answers.

Fewer questions allowed to stay visible.

Busy again.

Busy enough to avoid the pause.

Pause deferred.

Deferred into tomorrow.

Tomorrow filled.

Filled before it starts.

Judgment waits.

It does not leave.

It does not interrupt.

It waits.

A fast day can hide a long drift.

A full calendar can hide a thin direction.

A completed list can hide an unanswered frame.

Nothing breaks.

So nothing interrupts the pattern.

The pattern keeps itself.

Response creates relief.

Relief rewards response.

Reward repeats response.

A quiet loop.

Not loud.

Not dramatic.

Just effective enough.

Just visible enough.

Just familiar enough.

The system works.

The system costs.

The cost distributes.

Small.

Then small again.

Hard to name while moving.

Easy to postpone while moving.

Movement fills the whole foreground.

Direction stays in the background.

Background questions.

Foreground tasks.

Foreground wins.

Again.

Again.

Again.

No collapse.

No reset.

Only accumulation.

A little more tolerance.

A little less friction noticed.

A little less pause available.

Judgment waits.

Still waiting.

Not absent.

Not active.

Near.

Deferred.

The day closes with motion.

The day opens with motion.

Between them,

one thin interval.

Often filled.

Often gone.

Still the same line returns:

The system works.

The system costs.

And below that,

another line:

judgment waits.

Not a turning point.

Just another day with answers.

Another day with speed.

Another day where speed looks like clarity.

Judgment waits.

The wait lengthens.

The work continues.

Nothing breaks.

The structure keeps its shape.

Questions stay near the edge.

Tasks stay in the center.

Center first.

Edge later.

Later postponed.

Postponed again.

The system works.

The system costs.

No announcement.

No interruption.

Only the same quiet substitution,

still in place.

Activity in front.

Judgment behind.

Visible motion.

Deferred direction.

And the same line,

without emphasis:

judgment waits.

Another quiet day.

Another completed list.

Another unasked frame question.

The pace holds.

The pause does not.

Judgment waits.

No signal changes.

No tone changes.

Only repetition.

Only motion.

Only the same soft exchange:

response now,

reflection later.

Later stays later.

The system works.

The system costs.

Nothing breaks.

And still

judgment waits.

Chapter 11

The Cost of Postponed Judgment

When judgment is delayed, it does not disappear.

It accumulates.

People often tell themselves that they will think later. When the pressure eases. When the workload lightens. When the timing is better.

This promise feels reasonable. It allows continuation without denial. Judgment is acknowledged, just deferred.

The problem is not delay itself. The problem is accumulation.

Each postponed evaluation adds weight. Questions stack. Uncertainty thickens.

Because judgment has not been exercised, conditions continue to change. New commitments form. Expectations adjust. Dependencies deepen.

By the time judgment returns, it faces a different situation.

This difference is rarely recognized. People assume they are revisiting the same decision.

In reality, they are evaluating a structure that has grown around the absence of judgment.

Postponement feels harmless in the moment. Nothing bad happens immediately. Work continues. Life remains functional.

But the cost of postponement is not immediate. It is structural.

Delayed judgment allows systems to settle without review. What emerges is not necessarily wrong, but it is unexamined.

Unexamined structures acquire inertia. They normalize themselves. They define what is reasonable.

When judgment finally engages, it encounters resistance. Not opposition, but density.

There is more to consider. More to disrupt. More to explain.

This density makes judgment harder. It demands more courage, more clarity, more energy.

Ironically, the longer judgment is postponed, the more intimidating it becomes.

People interpret this intimidation as a sign that judgment is dangerous. They assume that thinking seriously now would create instability.

In fact, the instability already exists. It has simply been absorbed gradually.

Postponement spreads cost over time. It avoids spikes. It keeps things manageable.

But it also ensures that no clear moment of evaluation arrives.

Each day of continuation feels too small to justify stopping. Each addition feels incremental.

This incrementalism traps judgment. There is never a good time.

People wait for certainty. They wait for exhaustion. They wait for permission.

Permission rarely comes.

Because the system is functioning, there is no external trigger. Because continuation is normalized, there is no obvious breakpoint.

Judgment remains deferred, not because it is forbidden, but because it is inconvenient.

This inconvenience grows.

Judgment requires confronting what has been allowed to form. It requires naming dependencies. It requires acknowledging limits.

These acknowledgments feel heavier the longer they are avoided.

Eventually, people describe themselves as stuck. They feel unable to decide, even though they have decided many times.

What they mean is not that judgment is gone. It is that judgment has become overwhelming.

This overwhelm is the true cost of postponement.

Had judgment been exercised earlier, it would have faced less complexity. Had evaluation been continuous, it would have remained manageable.

Postponement concentrates difficulty.

This does not imply regret. It does not accuse anyone of negligence. It simply explains why judgment can feel harder than it should.

The difficulty is not inherent. It is accumulated.

Understanding this reframes the problem. The issue is not that judgment failed. It is that judgment waited.

Waiting was adaptive. It allowed continuation. It preserved stability.

But adaptation has consequences.

Judgment delayed does not return unchanged. It returns burdened.

Recognizing this does not demand immediate action. It restores context.

The weight you feel is not proof of danger. It is evidence of accumulation.

Accumulation can be addressed, but it cannot be undone instantly.

This is why judgment often returns slowly. Not as a decision, but as a gradual reappearance of perspective.

That reappearance is not dramatic. It does not resolve everything.

It simply marks the end of indefinite postponement.

From here, judgment does not need to rush. It only needs to be allowed back into time. A familiar sequence starts with a small doubt that seems too minor for immediate review. The day is full, obligations are active, and postponing evaluation appears harmless. The doubt is noted mentally, then set aside until a quieter period. A quieter period does not arrive that week. The same decision environment continues, and new inputs are added on top of the unresolved question. Postponement remains reasonable in each moment because nothing has yet failed visibly.

In project work, this can look like repeated short deferrals of strategic review. Teams continue shipping, fixing, and coordinating while telling themselves that deeper assessment will happen after the next release. The release arrives with new tasks attached. Another deferral follows. Over several cycles, the project becomes more complex, with additional integrations, commitments, and stakeholders. By the time review is attempted, the scope of what must be evaluated is much larger than when the first doubt appeared.

A similar dynamic appears in personal life when someone postpones a difficult conversation. Timing never feels ideal. There is always a practical reason to wait: travel schedules, work deadlines, family events, a period of fatigue. Waiting prevents immediate disruption and preserves daily function. Meanwhile, assumptions harden. Behaviors adjust around what remains unsaid. The eventual conversation, when it occurs, must address not only the original issue but the architecture formed during delay.

Postponed judgment often accumulates quietly because each deferral is framed as temporary. Temporary language lowers alarm and preserves continuity. "Not now" sounds contained. Repeated over months, "not now" becomes an operating principle. Decisions continue to be made in the absence of explicit evaluation. The system adapts to that absence by building around it. Adaptation can be efficient in the short term, but it increases the amount that must later be understood simultaneously.

Hesitation before judgment is strengthened by this increasing density. People sense that proper evaluation now requires time, co-ordination, and emotional capacity they do not currently have. Since those resources are scarce, they postpone again. The postponement reduces immediate pressure and reinforces the belief that waiting is pragmatic. The unresolved material does not disappear; it changes shape, spreads across contexts, and becomes harder to isolate as a single decision point.

In organizations, postponed judgment can be seen in policy drift. Temporary exceptions are granted to keep operations moving. Each exception is rational in context. Over time, exceptions interact and form a de facto policy that no one has explicitly reviewed. Staff adapt to the emergent pattern. New hires learn it as normal practice. When formal review is finally proposed, the question is no longer whether one exception made sense. The question is how to evaluate an entire structure produced by accumulated deferral.

The emotional tone of this process is usually moderate rather than dramatic. People are often calm, competent, and sincere while postponing judgment. They are not necessarily avoiding reality; they are prioritizing immediate manageability. This makes the eventual burden more confusing. When evaluation finally returns, the load feels disproportionate to any single deferred moment. The disproportion is real because the burden reflects accumulation across many moments, not the significance of one event.

Temporal delay also alters memory. Earlier conditions become less accessible, and people underestimate how much simpler judgment once would have been. The present complexity feels normal because it was built gradually. Looking back, the path appears continuous, and no single fork stands out. This continuity obscures the compounding effect of postponement. Without a clear marker, individuals may interpret current difficulty as personal indecision rather than as structural density generated over time.

In creative work, postponed judgment can appear as endless refinement without periodic reassessment of direction. Drafts improve at the sentence level while the core question remains unexamined. Each revision deepens attachment and increases sunk time. Reassessment feels more expensive later because so much detail has been developed under initial assumptions. The creator senses misalignment yet delays confronting it, preferring another pass that keeps movement visible. Visibility of movement substitutes for clarity of direction.

Another repeated scene involves calendar management. Reflection sessions are scheduled, then displaced by urgent items. The displacement is understandable and often necessary. What matters is repetition. Repeated displacement communicates, implicitly, that judgment has lower priority than response. Over months, response culture dominates. People become excellent at handling incoming demands and less practiced at evaluating the structure generating those demands. Judgment returns as a heavier task because the muscle of timely evaluation has been underused.

Social dynamics amplify postponement. When groups are co-ordinated around momentum, raising foundational questions can feel untimely or disruptive. Individuals defer concerns to preserve harmony and pace. Others do the same. Silence is interpreted as alignment, and momentum continues. Later, when questions surface, participants may be surprised by their scale. The scale reflects collective accumulation of private postponements. No one intended this outcome, but distributed deferral produced it anyway.

In personal commitments, postponed judgment can create a sensation of being trapped without obvious external constraints. People may still have options, yet every option now touches multiple dependencies that formed during delay. A simple choice has become a multi-system choice. This does not eliminate freedom, but it raises decision cost. Higher cost encourages further postponement, creating a loop where delay increases complexity and complexity increases delay.

The language used during this phase often remains practical: "after this cycle," "once things settle," "when bandwidth improves." These phrases are not deceptive. They reflect real constraints. At the same time, they can function as stabilizers for indefinite deferral.

Because future conditions are uncertain, each phrase is perpetually renewable. Judgment is always planned and rarely instantiated. The gap between intent and execution widens gradually, then becomes a standing feature of the system.

Across contexts, the structure repeats: a question is deferred, operations continue, dependencies grow, and deferred evaluation returns with greater weight. The return is slower than expected because the material is denser than before. People spend time mapping what formed during postponement before they can evaluate what to do about it. Mapping itself feels like work without outcome, which can tempt another round of delay. The cycle can extend without clear endpoint.

No final resolution appears in this stage. Work proceeds, commitments remain active, and judgment re-enters in fragments rather than as a single decisive event. One concern is named, then another, while daily operations continue in parallel. The structural cost of postponement becomes visible gradually, through increased effort required simply to understand the present. Understanding grows, but so does awareness of how much accumulated material still awaits review.

The chapter of postponed judgment therefore remains open. Conditions are not static, yet neither are they fully evaluated. People continue to function within arrangements shaped by prior delay, noticing more as time passes, and carrying the unresolved task of judgment alongside the ordinary demands that initially made postponement seem like the reasonable choice.

Postponed judgment can also be institutionalized through reporting cycles. Teams report status frequently and strategy infrequently. Frequent status updates create a sense of control because activity is visible and measurable. Strategic questions that do not fit status templates are deferred to quarterly or annual windows. When those windows arrive, urgent status demands still dominate attention. Strategy review is shortened, postponed, or translated back into operational language. The system appears responsive while foundational evaluation remains underdeveloped.

In personal contexts, postponement often hides inside productivity. A person becomes highly efficient at handling incoming demands and receives positive feedback for responsiveness. Responsiveness reduces immediate stress and strengthens identity as someone dependable under pressure. The unresolved judgments beneath this performance receive less time because available attention is consumed by maintaining responsiveness. Efficiency and postponement coexist, making delay appear compatible with competence.

Another repeated scene involves partial decisions that stand in for full judgment. Someone adjusts a timeline, modifies a scope, or renegotiates a minor expectation. These moves reduce pressure temporarily and create the impression that core issues are being addressed. Often they are not. Core evaluation remains deferred while peripheral adjustments accumulate. Over time, the periphery becomes dense, and distinguishing symptom management from structural review becomes harder.

Temporal accumulation changes the emotional profile of judgment when it eventually returns. What began as a manageable question now touches many people, commitments, and narratives. The person engaging judgment feels disproportionate resistance not because judgment is inherently dangerous, but because delay allowed interdependencies to multiply. Multiplication raises stakes and prolongs evaluation, which can encourage another round of postponement.

In group settings, postponed judgment can become a shared etiquette. Members avoid raising deep concerns in forums optimized for forward motion. Concerns are deferred to private conversations, where each participant assumes someone else may raise them later. Later often does not arrive in collective form. The group continues effectively on short horizons while long-horizon coherence remains largely unexamined.

No dramatic failure is required for this condition to persist. Systems can function competently while carrying substantial deferred judgment. Functioning delays urgency, and delayed urgency delays evaluation. The cycle can run across long intervals, producing growing complexity that becomes visible only when someone attempts to map the whole structure.

When mapping begins, progress is slow. Threads are traced, assumptions surfaced, and old deferrals rediscovered in current constraints. Daily obligations continue in parallel, limiting available capacity for sustained review. Judgment returns in segments, pauses, then returns again. The process remains open, with accumulation still present and full evaluation still in progress.

As postponed judgment accumulates, people can become highly skilled at operating within complexity they did not deliberately choose. Skill keeps the system functional, and functionality delays full review again. The delay is not irrational; it is often the only way daily obligations remain manageable. Still, each interval of manageability is purchased by carrying unresolved evaluation forward.

The result is a prolonged middle state: decisions are continuously made, while foundational judgment remains partially deferred. The structure holds, and the backlog of interpretation remains active in the background.

In this way, postponement remains adaptive and costly at the same time. It protects immediate function while increasing future interpretive load. The load is rarely visible all at once; it appears as recurring difficulty whenever deeper evaluation is attempted.

The process therefore continues in layers: ongoing execution above, accumulated judgment below, and intermittent attempts to reconnect the two.

Even with this burden, ordinary routines continue to function, which keeps postponement plausible and judgment partially deferred. The chapter remains one of accumulation in motion: operational continuity above, unresolved evaluation below.

Because this layered state can remain functional, it can also remain in place for extended periods. Postponed judgment does not halt the system; it travels with the system, adding interpretive weight while ordinary execution continues.

Chapter 12

When Clarity Does Not Bring Relief

People often expect clarity to feel good.

They imagine that once things are understood, relief will follow. Tension will drop. Confidence will return.

When this does not happen, they assume something is wrong.

In reality, clarity often feels uncomfortable first.

This discomfort surprises people because it contradicts expectation. Understanding is supposed to simplify. Instead, it complicates.

The complication comes from contrast.

Before clarity, effort filled the space. Continuation justified itself. Busyness absorbed uncertainty.

These activities created movement. Movement created momentum. Momentum reduced awareness.

When judgment returns, momentum slows. Space opens.

In that space, things become visible.

Visibility does not resolve anything. It exposes.

What is exposed is not disaster. It is misalignment.

Misalignment is subtle. It is not a single mistake. It is a pattern that no longer fits cleanly.

Seeing this pattern does not immediately suggest action. It creates tension.

The tension comes from holding two truths at once. The system works. The system costs.

Previously, these truths were separated by activity. Now they coexist.

Coexistence is uncomfortable.

People often misinterpret this discomfort. They assume clarity has increased risk. They believe that thinking has made things worse.

In fact, clarity has removed anesthesia.

Anesthesia numbed friction. It softened edges. It blurred contradictions.

Without it, sensations sharpen.

This sharpening feels like danger, but it is awareness.

Awareness lacks momentum. It does not push. It does not pull.

It simply holds.

Holding is demanding. It requires tolerance. It resists closure.

Many people rush to end this state. They look for conclusions. They seek decisions. They want relief.

Relief often arrives through action. Action restores momentum. Momentum narrows perception.

This is why clarity is often followed by overreaction. People mistake exposure for emergency.

They act not because they know what to do, but because they want the discomfort to stop.

Understanding this pattern matters. It prevents mislabeling clarity as failure.

The unease that follows judgment is not evidence that judgment is wrong. It is evidence that judgment is active.

Judgment disrupts habits. It interrupts flow. It suspends justification.

Suspension feels unstable because it lacks narrative.

Before, continuation provided a story. Effort made sense. Busyness explained everything.

Clarity removes the story before offering a replacement.

This gap is where discomfort lives.

Nothing has to fill it immediately. But people often believe it must.

They search for direction not because they are lost, but because they are newly aware.

Awareness without direction feels incomplete. It invites impatience.

This impatience is understandable. It reflects a desire for coherence.

But coherence does not arrive on demand. It forms gradually.

Rushing it risks replacing one structure with another equally unexamined.

Clarity is not a solution. It is a condition.

It allows evaluation. It does not provide outcome.

When clarity appears, many people try to convert it into certainty. They want to know what it means.

Meaning comes later. Sometimes much later.

In the meantime, clarity asks for tolerance. Tolerance of ambiguity. Tolerance of unresolved tension.

This tolerance is rare because it is not rewarded.

Others expect answers. Systems prefer decisions. Momentum favors movement.

Clarity resists all three.

It does not answer. It does not decide. It does not move.

This resistance is not stubbornness. It is fidelity.

Fidelity to what is seen, rather than what is expected.

Understanding this reframes discomfort. The unease is not a signal to act. It is a signal to remain present.

Presence is not passive. It is attentive without urgency.

This state is unfamiliar because most environments do not support it.

People leave it too quickly, not because it is harmful, but because it is quiet.

Quiet can feel empty after long periods of noise.

In truth, it is full.

It holds everything that was previously drowned out.

Clarity does not bring relief because relief belongs to resolution.

Clarity brings honesty.

Honesty is heavier, but it is also more stable.

From here, judgment does not need to rush.

It has returned. That is enough for now.

This judgment can be restated without changing its contour. Clarity is not the same as comfort. Clarity is not the same as ease. Clarity is not the same as relief. Clarity can coexist with strain. Clarity can coexist with tension. Clarity can coexist with unresolved pressure.

To say this slowly: the arrival of clearer perception does not guarantee a reduction in felt weight. Perception can sharpen while the felt field becomes heavier. The heavier feeling does not cancel the sharper perception. The heavier feeling can be produced by that sharpened perception.

This is not a contradiction that needs repair. It is a boundary against a common misreading. The misreading says that discomfort after clarity proves that clarity has failed. This chapter refuses that equivalence. Discomfort after clarity can indicate that numbing has decreased, not that understanding has disappeared.

Another phrasing keeps the same center. Clarity does not sedate. Clarity discloses. Disclosure can be quiet and still difficult. Disclosure can be accurate and still unpleasant. Disclosure can reduce confusion while increasing contact with what confusion had softened.

This is not a claim that discomfort is desirable. It is not an elevation of pain. It is not a romanticization of difficulty. It is a descriptive line: relief is not the defining signal of genuine clarity.

Relief often belongs to closure. Clarity can appear before closure. Clarity can remain present in the absence of closure. Where closure is absent, relief may also be absent. The absence of relief does not remove the clarity already present.

The same judgment can be framed through negation. This is not emotional failure. This is not interpretive error. This is not evidence that one has thought incorrectly. It is not evidence that one must return to noise in order to feel stable.

Another boundary matters. This chapter does not claim that every discomfort is clarity. Discomfort is not automatically insight. The point is narrower: discomfort is not sufficient evidence against insight. The two can coincide without canceling each other.

The sentence can be restated in terms of sequence. Noise can suppress friction. Clarity can remove suppression. When suppression lowers, friction becomes newly felt. The felt increase does not necessarily indicate a real increase in friction. It can indicate reduced insulation from friction that was already present.

This framing does not explain away intensity. It locates intensity differently. Intensity can shift from external demand to internal contact. External demand may remain similar while internal contact deepens. The resulting unease is not fabricated. It is an effect of closer proximity to what had been buffered.

The judgment can also be stated as a distinction between direction and sensation. Clarity concerns direction of seeing. Relief concerns sensation of burden. Direction and sensation are related but not identical. A change in one does not guarantee an immediate change in the other.

This is not a call to preserve discomfort. It is not a call to reject comfort. It is not a call to mistrust any form of easing. It is a refusal to use comfort as a sole criterion of interpretive validity.

Another rephrasing: Clarity can increase definition without increasing consolation. Clarity can reduce ambiguity about what is present without reducing the cost of what is present. Clarity can remove false hope and thereby remove a temporary source of calm. The removal can feel like worsening. The structure may be that accuracy has increased.

The thought can be repeated with emphasis on timing. Relief can be delayed. Recognition can be immediate. The delay is not a defect in recognition. The delay is part of what recognition alters. Recognition changes relation first. Relief, if it arrives, belongs to a later and separate movement.

This is not an argument for rushing toward answers. Answer-seeking can restore comfort by compressing complexity. Compression can produce immediate calm while distorting proportion. The chapter keeps this possibility visible without turning it into instruction.

Another boundary reduces a different misreading. The claim is not that clarity must hurt. The claim is that hurt does not disprove clarity. The claim is not that understanding should remain unresolved forever. The claim is that unresolvedness is compatible with understanding.

The statement can be placed in semantic distance. Clarity is a change in fidelity. Relief is a change in pressure. Fidelity can rise while pressure remains. Pressure can remain while narrative certainty falls. Narrative certainty can fall because fidelity has increased.

This is not therapeutic language. It does not assign stages. It does not assign outcomes. It does not assign proper emotional responses. It holds one anchor proposition against premature interpretation.

That proposition can be repeated as a line of boundaries. Clarity is not reassurance. Clarity is not closure. Clarity is not motivation. Clarity is not a reward state. Clarity is contact with what is there, including what remains unresolved.

The same line can be restated through what clarity is not required to do. Clarity is not required to remove tension. Clarity is not required to provide immediate orientation toward action. Clarity is not required to generate social legibility. Clarity is not required to feel good in order to remain valid.

Another phrasing keeps the idea from collapsing into guidance. This chapter does not prescribe tolerance. It names a condition where tolerance is often demanded by the condition itself. The naming is descriptive, not directive. The chapter does not convert discomfort into duty.

The judgment can also be framed as protection against a specific shortcut. Shortcut: if it feels worse, it must be wrong. Counter-anchor: it can feel worse because what was blurred is now less blurred. The anchor does not eliminate ambiguity. It prevents one rapid verdict from dominating interpretation.

A further boundary: This is not a technique for producing clarity. This is not a sequence for stabilizing clarity. This is not a framework for evaluating emotions. It is a repeated sentence in different forms so that one misreading loses automatic authority.

The sentence in another form: The return of judgment can strip away compensatory momentum. When compensation thins, raw proportion becomes visible. Raw proportion can be heavier than compensated proportion. Heaviness here is not necessarily danger. It is unbuffered contact.

This does not mean buffering is always false. Buffering can sustain function. Buffering can preserve continuity. The chapter does not condemn buffering. It distinguishes buffering from clarity. The two can coexist, and the reduction of one can reveal the other.

Another re-statement through rhythm. Before clarity, pressure may move fast and feel familiar. With clarity, pressure may move slower and feel sharper. Familiar acceleration can feel safer than unfamiliar stillness. Safety-feeling and validity-feeling can diverge. The divergence itself is part of the judgment.

This is not a claim about any single emotion. Anxiety, quiet, restlessness, heaviness, and neutrality can all appear. No single affect validates or invalidates clarity on its own. The chapter resists one-to-one mapping between feeling tone and epistemic status.

Another boundary statement: The judgment is not anti-relief. Relief may come. Relief may not come. Clarity does not depend on the schedule of relief. The schedule of relief is not the measure of whether clarity has appeared.

The same meaning can be written in terms of exposure. Exposure is not conclusion. Exposure is not instruction. Exposure is contact. Contact can remain open. Open contact can feel unresolved. Unresolved contact can still be accurate.

This is not a project of certainty. Certainty can lower discomfort quickly. Lower discomfort can be mistaken for truth. Truth here is not framed as certainty. Truth here is framed as less distortion. Less distortion can carry more immediate weight.

Another rephrase against a common collapse. If clarity does not immediately simplify, clarity is not therefore absent. If clarity does not immediately soothe, clarity is not therefore false. If clarity does not immediately point forward, clarity is not therefore useless. These equivalences are declined.

The chapter can be heard as an anti-equation. Understanding does not equal relief. Understanding does not equal readiness. Understanding does not equal reduced burden. Understanding can equal increased precision about burden.

This does not produce a neat endpoint. The ambiguity remains. Relief may follow later. Relief may appear in fragments. Relief may appear in different forms than expected. None of these outcomes are stabilized here as rule.

Another boundary clarifies what this is not trying to become. This is not a defense of endless suspension. This is not a refusal of eventual decision. This is not an argument against movement. It is an anchor against mislabeling early discomfort as invalidation.

The same judgment in quieter terms: Clarity can feel heavy because it removes borrowed narratives. Borrowed narratives can provide temporary comfort. When borrowed narratives thin, burden may feel less mediated. This is not regression. This can be increased proximity to what had already been true.

This is not a heroic account. No triumph language is needed. No breakthrough language is needed. The chapter avoids dramatic conversion. It holds a low-intensity proposition across many phrasings so it is harder to mishear.

That proposition again: Relief is not the criterion. Pleasantness is not the criterion. Immediate coherence is not the criterion. The criterion here is reduced distortion, even when reduced distortion arrives with unease.

Another boundary against moralization. Feeling discomfort after clarity is not weakness. Feeling discomfort after clarity is not failure of discipline. Feeling discomfort after clarity is not proof of insufficient maturity. These moral readings are outside the anchor.

Another boundary against instrumentalization. The chapter does not turn discomfort into a productivity asset. It does not frame unease as fuel. It does not redirect tension toward performance. It only keeps the judgment from being dismissed because it is not consoling.

The same line in semantic distance: Clarity changes the ratio between narrative and perception. When narrative decreases faster than perception stabilizes, disquiet can rise. The rise does not negate the change. It describes the transitional relation between these terms.

This remains a definition anchor. It does not seek to settle the whole field. It seeks to preserve one careful distinction long enough to prevent collapse into a single reflexive reading. That distinction: discomfort is compatible with clarity. Discomfort can even be a local effect of clarity.

Another repetition with altered cadence. Clarity may not soothe. Clarity may not simplify. Clarity may not direct. Clarity may still be clarity.

Another repetition through exclusions. Not guidance. Not method. Not application. Not closure. Only a sustained effort to keep one judgment from being translated too quickly into its opposite.

And again, without escalation. When relief does not follow, nothing has necessarily gone wrong. When tension remains, nothing has necessarily failed. When ambiguity persists, nothing has necessarily been lost. What may have appeared is a less padded contact with what is already there.

The sentence can rest here without final answer. Clarity does not bring relief. The statement remains incomplete on purpose. It does not decide what follows. It does not decide what should follow. It leaves open what remains open while resisting the misreading that openness proves absence.

Clarity can be reformulated as reduced distortion without promised consolation. Reduced distortion and consolation are not equivalent outputs. Consolation can lag. Consolation can fail to appear. The absence of consolation does not reinstall the prior distortion by itself.

This is not a demand to remain in discomfort. The chapter does not demand any affective posture. It only prevents one inference from becoming automatic: no relief therefore no clarity. That inference is too narrow for the structure being named.

Another version of the same boundary: Immediate calm is not a reliability test for perception. Immediate calm can result from simplification. Simplification can obscure proportion. Clarity can feel less calm precisely because simplification has been reduced.

This does not imply superiority of unease. Unease is not elevated. Unease is not canonized. It is simply decoupled from failure. Decoupling is the anchor.

The thought can be repeated through a semantic split. Perceptual resolution and emotional resolution can move at different speeds. Speed mismatch can feel like contradiction. The contradiction is often temporal, not logical. Temporal mismatch does not negate either side.

Another boundary against premature closure: If discomfort remains, no immediate verdict follows. Discomfort does not force action. Discomfort does not force regression. Discomfort does not force interpretive reversal. It can mark continued contact with unresolved proportion.

This is not a method of waiting. No sequence is implied. No tactic is encoded. Only a refusal to convert discomfort into disproof.

Another restatement with less explanation. Clarity can clarify burden, not remove burden. Clarity can clarify cost, not cancel cost. Clarity can clarify tension, not terminate tension. The clarification itself is the event being named.

Again through negation. Not confusion because uneasy. Not error because unresolved. Not failure because relief is absent. These equations are withheld.

Another phrasing: A clearer map does not flatten terrain. A clearer map can make steepness more visible. Visibility of steepness can feel heavier than blur. Heaviness here is compatible with improved map fidelity.

This is not didactic certainty. The chapter does not claim universal trajectories. It anchors a non-equivalence so that one recurring misread loses force.

That non-equivalence: pleasantness is not proof, unpleasantness is not disproof. The relation between feeling tone and judgment validity is underdetermined. The chapter keeps that underdetermination explicit.

Another boundary around interpretation speed. Quick meaning can reduce discomfort and reduce accuracy. Slow meaning can preserve discomfort and preserve accuracy. Neither pairing is absolute. The possibility matters enough to be named repeatedly.

This is not encouragement toward indecision. It is protection against false invalidation. Protection here is linguistic. If language ties clarity to relief too tightly, clarity is dismissed whenever relief is delayed. The anchor loosens that tie.

Another restatement: Clarity can destabilize compensatory narratives. Destabilized narratives can remove temporary equilibrium. Removed equilibrium can be felt as worsening. Worsening-feel is not identical to worsening-structure.

This does not deny that structures can worsen. It denies a shortcut from sensation to verdict. The shortcut is the misinterpretation being reduced.

Again in minimal terms. Clearer does not mean easier. Clearer does not mean lighter. Clearer can mean sharper. Sharper can mean heavier. Heavier can still be truer.

Another boundary against translation into guidance. No recommendation follows from this sentence alone. No procedure follows from this sentence alone. No application schema is implied. The sentence remains definitional.

The definition can be repeated one more time. Clarity does not bring relief is not pessimism. It is not optimism either. It is a boundary statement about what clarity is not required to provide.

The same anchor, quiet and open: Clarity can remain present while discomfort remains present. Both can coexist without one invalidating the other. No further closure is added here.

Another boundary can be stated plainly. The chapter does not seek consolation language. It seeks misreading resistance. If clarity is tied only to relief, clarity will be denied whenever relief is late. This anchor keeps that denial from becoming automatic.

So the sentence remains unclosed. Clarity does not bring relief. It is not a slogan for despair and not a promise of eventual ease. It is a definition that keeps perception and comfort from being falsely merged.

Chapter 13

Why Judgment Does Not Require Immediate Action

When judgment returns, many people assume action must follow.

They feel an internal pressure to do something with what they now see. Understanding seems incomplete without response.

This assumption is deeply learned. In most environments, evaluation exists to enable action. Thinking is justified by outcome.

When outcome does not appear, judgment feels unfinished.

But judgment does not operate on the same timeline as action.

Judgment observes. Action intervenes.

Observation can remain valid without intervention. Seeing clearly does not obligate movement.

This distinction is unfamiliar because it is rarely supported.

Systems reward decisiveness. They value resolution. They prefer closure.

Judgment resists closure. It holds complexity. It notices contradiction.

When contradiction is seen, action often feels like relief. Doing something simplifies the picture. It collapses uncertainty into direction.

This collapse is tempting, especially after long periods of confusion.

But collapse is not always clarification. Sometimes it is avoidance.

Judgment requires space to settle. It needs time without demand. It needs freedom from justification.

Immediate action interrupts this settling. It replaces evaluation with execution.

Execution produces movement. Movement feels productive. Productivity reassures.

Reassurance is not the same as alignment.

Many people mistake the absence of action for indecision. They interpret waiting as weakness.

In reality, waiting can be a form of integrity.

Integrity here does not mean virtue. It means coherence between perception and response.

If perception has widened, response does not need to narrow immediately.

Judgment that is rushed often re-enters old patterns. It reaches for familiar solutions. It repeats previous logic.

This repetition restores comfort without honoring what has changed.

Allowing judgment to exist without action feels risky because it removes distraction.

There is nothing to point to. No progress to show. No explanation to offer.

This absence creates exposure.

Exposure is uncomfortable in cultures that equate value with output.

People fear being seen as inactive. They fear wasting time. They fear losing momentum.

Momentum has carried them this far. Letting it slow feels dangerous.

But momentum is not neutral. It has direction. It carries assumptions.

When judgment returns, it often questions those assumptions.

Acting immediately can protect momentum at the expense of evaluation.

This protection feels responsible. It maintains continuity. It avoids disruption.

But it also postpones reckoning.

Judgment does not demand urgency. It demands honesty.

Honesty can exist without movement. It can remain present while outcomes remain undecided.

This presence changes the internal experience. Pressure reduces. Noise subsides. Perspective widens.

None of this requires action. In fact, action often short-circuits it.

People who allow judgment to rest often describe a strange calm. Not relief, but steadiness.

This steadiness is fragile. It does not announce itself. It can be easily overridden.

External demands return. Internal habits resurface.

The urge to act reappears.

Understanding the difference between judgment and action allows that urge to be examined.

Do I need to respond, or do I need to see more?

This question is not a method. It is a pause.

Pauses are undervalued because they do not produce artifacts.

But pauses create proportion. They prevent premature closure.

Judgment that is allowed to linger often deepens. It notices connections missed before. It recontextualizes earlier concerns.

This deepening cannot be scheduled. It unfolds unevenly.

Trying to force it into action reduces its scope.

Judgment does not promise answers. It promises orientation.

Orientation can exist before direction is chosen.

In that orientation, action regains legitimacy. Not as a reflex, but as a response.

Until then, judgment does not need to justify itself.

It is already doing its work by being present.

Action can wait.

Waiting is not failure. It is restraint.

Restraint allows judgment to complete itself before being translated into movement.

A recurring scene begins after a period of internal clarification. The person now sees patterns more distinctly, yet external routines continue in familiar form. Meetings remain scheduled, messages still require replies, and commitments continue to arrive. Nothing in the environment requires an immediate declaration. In this space, judgment is active but unannounced. It influences what is noticed, what is questioned internally, and what is no longer assumed. Action, however, stays largely unchanged for a while.

This interval is often misunderstood by observers because visibility is low. From outside, continuity suggests that nothing significant has shifted. From inside, continuity coexists with a different orientation. The person may listen differently in conversations, tracking inconsistencies that previously passed unnoticed. They may decline to reinforce narratives that once felt automatic, even while still participating in routine exchanges. These are small positional adjustments rather than overt moves, and they do not immediately produce measurable outcomes.

In organizational contexts, judgment without immediate action can appear as a leader who stops making automatic commitments. Requests still receive responses, but responses include more silence before agreement, more clarification before timelines, and fewer reflexive assurances. The calendar looks similar for several weeks. The underlying stance is not similar. The leader is no longer operating from inherited momentum alone. Still, no dramatic announcement is made, and operations continue while this changed stance stabilizes.

A parallel scene appears in personal relationships. Someone recognizes a recurring pattern and refrains from instantly correcting it through confrontation or withdrawal. Interactions proceed with subtle shifts in attention. Certain topics are no longer bypassed internally, even if they are not yet raised externally. The person observes more and reacts less. This can look like passivity to others and feel like restraint to the person involved. The distinction remains private and unresolved for some time.

Hesitation before action is not always uncertainty about what is seen. Often it is uncertainty about timing, scope, and consequence of intervention. The person may understand the pattern clearly and still sense that immediate movement would collapse complexity into a premature gesture. Waiting is therefore not absence of judgment. It is coexistence with judgment while refusing to force rapid translation into behavior that cannot yet carry the full weight of what has been noticed.

Temporal delay is central here. Orientation tends to settle in layers. An initial recognition is followed by secondary recognitions that contextualize it. Earlier assumptions are revisited and reinterpreted. What first looked like a single issue may reveal links to role expectations, institutional incentives, or long-standing habits. If action occurs too quickly, these links can remain unintegrated. By delaying action, the person allows additional layers to surface, even as daily life continues around them.

In professional teams, this phase may involve reduced participation in performative urgency. A person still attends high-pressure sessions but contributes with narrower claims and fewer sweeping commitments. They do not oppose momentum directly; they stop amplifying it. The difference is easy to miss in real time. Over months, it changes interaction patterns subtly. Colleagues may notice that the person is harder to recruit into reactive cycles, though no explicit boundary-setting event has occurred yet.

Judgment without immediate action can feel exposed because it lacks artifacts. There is no new plan to display, no decisive announcement, no visible metric proving progress. Output-oriented cultures often interpret artifact absence as inactivity. The person feels this interpretive pressure while choosing not to produce symbolic movement for reassurance. Routine tasks continue, but the internal center of gravity has shifted from performance of decisiveness to maintenance of accurate perception.

Another repeated scene is private review. Notes are revisited, conversations mentally replayed, and subtle patterns are compared across time. The person is not collecting evidence for a courtroom-style conclusion; they are allowing orientation to become less fragile. Early clarity can be sharp but unstable. Additional observation gives it texture. Texture reduces the likelihood that action will merely repeat old dynamics under new language. No final threshold is obvious. Stabilization happens gradually and unevenly.

In institutions with strong momentum norms, this waiting phase may be masked by continued productivity. People keep delivering and meeting obligations while holding unresolved judgments in the background. Productivity protects social standing and buys temporal space for orientation to mature. The arrangement can persist for long periods. It is neither full endorsement of the status quo nor overt challenge to it. It is a middle position where judgment remains active and action remains intentionally incomplete.

Across contexts, misunderstanding frequently arises when others equate seeing with acting. They ask, implicitly or explicitly, what the person plans to do now that they see. The question assumes linear conversion from insight to intervention. Real processes are less linear. Insight may first alter interpretation, then pacing, then language, and only later visible commitments. The sequence can be hard to defend in environments that reward immediate clarity. The person may continue quietly rather than debate the legitimacy of delay.

The internal experience during this period can include alternating calm and impatience. Calm comes from reduced self-deception and clearer orientation. Impatience comes from living inside unchanged structures while perceiving them differently. Neither feeling settles the timeline. Days continue with ordinary obligations, and judgment stays present as a background organizer rather than a trigger for immediate external change. This dual condition may last longer than expected.

Repeated structure appears in many small moments: a message drafted and softened, a meeting point noted but not contested, a request accepted with narrower scope, a familiar argument heard without automatic defense. Each moment is minor. Together they indicate that judgment is influencing behavior at low amplitude. High-amplitude action has not arrived. The process remains in formation, and observation continues alongside participation.

No conclusion is required for this phase to remain meaningful. Orientation can remain valid while outward movement is delayed. Validity here is not measured by visible disruption but by sustained coherence between what is seen and what is no longer automatically reinforced. The person remains inside ongoing systems, neither fully reproducing prior patterns nor fully exiting them. Time passes, and the interval between judgment and action remains open.

In that open interval, pressure for closure returns repeatedly. New events invite quick interpretations, and social rhythms favor immediate response. Sometimes the person responds conventionally; sometimes they refrain. The pattern is mixed, not resolved. What persists is the refusal to treat judgment as incomplete merely because it has not yet been converted into decisive public movement.

The scene therefore continues without final turn: routines remain active, perception remains widened, and action remains partial. Judgment does not disappear in the absence of immediate intervention. It stays in circulation, shaping attention and pacing while the external world proceeds at its usual speed.

Judgment without immediate action often becomes visible first in pacing. A person who once answered instantly now allows requests to sit briefly before responding. The response may be similar in content, yet the interval changes what enters consideration. Additional context is noticed, implicit assumptions become clearer, and automatic escalation is less common. To others, this can look like minor delay. To the person, it is an operational sign that perception is being allowed to inform tempo before commitment is made.

In collaborative environments, this phase may involve selective participation in urgency loops. The person still contributes, still meets obligations, and still supports shared outcomes. What changes is willingness to supply momentum where rationale is weak. They no longer amplify every perceived emergency. This shift is modest and often unannounced. Because announcements are absent, peers may not register the underlying judgment, only occasional differences in intensity.

Another recurring scene is conversational. During discussions that once produced immediate agreement, the person now asks for clarification or leaves certain claims unendorsed. The meeting continues, and no overt conflict occurs. The absence of overt conflict can conceal meaningful change: old reflexes are not being fully reenacted. The person remains inside the structure while withholding automatic reinforcement of its faster patterns.

Temporal delay remains important because action taken too quickly can collapse nuanced perception into familiar scripts. Allowing judgment to persist without immediate translation creates a buffer where perception can mature. Maturation includes contradiction: seeing multiple valid constraints at once, noticing that clear orientation does not automatically reveal timing, and recognizing that external readiness may lag internal clarity. These recognitions are uncomfortable and often unspectacular.

In personal commitments, judgment without action can look like continued presence with altered interpretation. The person keeps appointments, honors promises, and maintains routines, yet no longer treats every demand as equally binding. Priorities begin to reorder internally before they are visible externally. Reordering can remain private for extended periods, especially when external disruption would generate noise unrelated to the quality of judgment itself.

Across these scenes, inactivity is an inaccurate label. Processes are active: observation deepens, assumptions are tested against repeated events, and language shifts gradually. What remains absent is decisive outward movement. The absence can persist without invalidating the process. It marks a phase where judgment is still unfolding in time and not yet condensed into a singular act.

The phase stays open. Daily operations continue, interpretation continues, and pressure for immediate conversion to action continues. None of these forces fully resolves the others. Judgment remains present and unfinalized, carrying coherence forward without demanding instant visible outcome.

In this interval, judgment continues doing quiet work even when no decisive action is visible. It filters interpretation, adjusts pacing, and limits automatic reenactment of prior patterns. These effects are incremental and easy to miss, but they alter how subsequent choices will be made when action eventually becomes legible.

Until that point, the chapter remains one of coexistence: active perception, partial participation, and delayed translation into overt change.

As this continues, judgment remains active without demanding immediate declaration. It keeps influencing interpretation and tempo while external structures proceed on familiar tracks. The absence of immediate action does not end the process; it extends the period where perception and behavior are held in careful, unresolved relation.

That unresolved relation can persist across ordinary weeks, with no climax and no final statement, while orientation continues to deepen in the background.

That coexistence can remain durable: clear internal orientation, continued external participation, and no immediate obligation to collapse one into the other.

Within this duration, judgment keeps shaping what is considered normal and what is no longer reinforced automatically. Visible action may still be limited, but orientation continues to alter the texture of participation in small, cumulative ways.

Chapter 14

When Judgment Becomes Legitimate Again

For a long time, judgment may have felt like a luxury.

Something you were allowed to do only after obligations were met. Only once everything else was handled. Only when pressure subsided.

Because pressure rarely subsides, judgment remained secondary.

It was squeezed between tasks. Interrupted by demands. Postponed until later.

When judgment begins to return, one of the first changes is subtle: it no longer needs permission.

This change is easy to overlook because nothing external shifts. Work may continue. Responsibilities remain.

What changes is internal posture.

Judgment no longer feels like indulgence. It no longer needs to justify its presence.

Before, thinking without acting felt irresponsible. You were supposed to produce something. You were supposed to show progress.

Now, judgment can exist without display.

This legitimacy reduces pressure. Not because problems are solved, but because evaluation is no longer constrained.

Constraint creates urgency. Urgency amplifies stress.

When judgment was constrained, it had to compete. It had to argue for space. It had to prove relevance.

That struggle was exhausting.

Once judgment is allowed, the struggle ends. Energy returns.

This return is often mistaken for relief. It is quieter than that. It feels like steadiness.

Steadiness comes from alignment, not resolution.

Alignment means perception and response are no longer in conflict. You are not forcing action against what you see.

This does not mean you stop acting. It means action no longer substitutes for evaluation.

Many people notice that their internal monologue changes. They stop explaining themselves in advance. They stop rehearsing justifications.

The need to defend thought disappears when thought is no longer treated as suspect.

This disappearance creates space. Space reduces noise. Noise reduction feels like calm.

Calm does not imply certainty. Uncertainty may still be present.

What is absent is panic.

Panic thrives on illegitimacy. It feeds on the fear that thinking alone is insufficient.

When judgment is legitimate, panic loses leverage.

This legitimacy also changes how pressure is interpreted. External demands still exist, but they are no longer internalized automatically.

Requests can be seen as requests, not commands.

Expectations can be noticed, not absorbed.

This distinction is subtle but transformative.

Previously, everything felt urgent because judgment had no standing. Now, urgency can be evaluated.

Evaluation does not require refusal. It requires recognition.

Recognition allows proportional response. Some things matter immediately. Others do not.

Judgment restores scale.

Scale reduces overwhelm. Overwhelm comes from flattening. When everything feels equally important, nothing can be assessed.

Judgment reintroduces hierarchy. Not imposed, but perceived.

This perception happens gradually. There is no sudden clarity. No dramatic shift.

Instead, pressure leaks out.

Moments that once triggered anxiety now feel tolerable. Delays that once felt dangerous now feel manageable.

This does not mean nothing is at stake. It means stakes are no longer inflated.

Inflation came from constraint. Constraint magnified consequence.

With judgment allowed, consequence returns to proportion.

People often worry that allowing judgment will lead to passivity. They fear becoming detached or inert.

This fear is understandable. They are used to equating pressure with engagement.

In reality, pressure and engagement are different.

Pressure forces attention. Engagement invites it.

Judgment supports engagement. It draws attention naturally.

When judgment is legitimate, attention becomes selective. Not everything demands focus.

This selectivity conserves energy. Conserved energy supports clarity.

Clarity does not compel action. It informs it.

From this position, doing nothing is not avoidance. It is choice deferred.

Deferral feels safe because judgment is present.

Presence replaces urgency.

This is not an endpoint. It is a condition.

A condition where judgment can breathe, without being rushed into decision.

That breathing space is where proportion stabilizes.

From here, nothing needs to be forced.

Judgment has returned to its place.

That return, by itself, changes everything.

From observer distance, legitimacy of judgment often appears first as a change in interaction tempo rather than declared philosophy. People pause longer before agreeing, treat incoming demands as inputs rather than commands, and leave some questions open without immediate self-correction. To close observers, these differences may look small. Across teams and over time, they alter how pressure circulates. Pressure still exists, but it is less likely to be absorbed instantly into identity-level obligation.

Institutional patterns support this reading. In groups where judgment regains standing, meetings can contain more unfilled space without being interpreted as failure of leadership or commitment. Participants still move work forward, but they do so with a wider tolerance for provisional language and partial visibility. Requests are mapped, not automatically internalized. This is not a dramatic cultural reset. It is a slow redistribution of authority from immediacy toward evaluation, visible mainly in repeated micro-sequences.

Time-delayed recognition is common because early phases look externally unchanged. Deliverables continue, responsibilities remain active, and no new doctrine is announced. Only later do participants notice that escalation patterns softened and that fewer issues were treated as existential by default. The recognition usually emerges in hindsight, when people compare periods and find that the same category of demand now generates less interpretive overload than before.

At system scale, legitimacy here means judgment no longer has to masquerade as output to be treated as real work. That shift reduces performative acceleration. Fewer explanatory loops are needed, fewer defensive commitments are made, and fewer tactical motions are used to prove engagement. None of this requires withdrawal from responsibility. It requires only that evaluation be allowed to remain visible without instant conversion into action symbols.

Quiet repetition reinforces the condition. Day after day, the environment continues to produce demands, and day after day, some demands are answered proportionally while others are held without alarm. The structure remains active, but the coupling between pressure and compulsion loosens. Over longer intervals, this loosening looks less like a decision and more like a new baseline for how judgment participates in ordinary coordination.

The chapter stays open inside that baseline. No final settlement is needed for the shift to remain operational: pressure continues, judgment remains legitimate within pressure, and recognition of the shift keeps arriving in delayed, low-intensity forms.

Observer accounts often emphasize how this legitimacy shift spreads socially without formal declaration. One person begins treating judgment as ordinary, then adjacent participants adjust by allowing slightly more interpretive space in shared tasks. Over time, the local norm changes from constant justification to proportional articulation. People still explain decisions when needed, but less explanatory effort is spent proving that judgment itself is permissible. The change is subtle and easier to detect in interaction transcripts than in official policy.

In complex systems, this shift can reduce secondary workload. When every reflective pause requires defense, participants generate additional communication to manage perceived hesitation. Once pauses are normalized, that extra communication shrinks. Meetings contain fewer preemptive disclaimers, fewer urgency amplifiers, and fewer symbolic commitments made mainly to demonstrate momentum. Operational throughput may remain similar, but interpretive overhead declines. Participants often notice this later as reduced background strain rather than as an explicit productivity gain.

Time-delayed recognition is common because the shift initially feels like mood variation. Teams may think they are simply in a lighter period. Only after similar demand levels return do they see that response quality changed in a durable way: fewer overreactions, fewer cascading escalations from minor disruptions, and more stable prioritization under pressure. External demands did not disappear. Internal processing of demand became less compressive.

At structural distance, legitimacy of judgment can be understood as a governance adjustment in attention allocation. Attention is no longer monopolized by immediacy signals. Some portion remains available for scale-setting and proportion checks during active periods, not only after breakdown. This does not eliminate urgency events. It changes how frequently urgency events redefine the whole environment.

Quiet repetition maintains the shift. Repeated days with ordinary pressure and ordinary evaluation gradually make the new posture unremarkable. What once felt like a special permission starts functioning as baseline practice. The system keeps moving, and judgment keeps occupying space inside that movement without needing constant defense.

Another perspective shift appears in how organizations remember pressure periods. Early memory often centers on volume: too many requests, too little time. Later memory, especially after comparison with similar volumes, centers on interpretation: how many requests were treated as totalizing, how many were treated proportionally, and how much judgment space remained during active demand. This delayed reframing changes what participants consider normal competence.

At system distance, legitimacy of judgment can therefore be tracked by what counts as an acceptable pause inside action-heavy intervals. Where pauses are interpreted as processing rather than hesitation, fewer secondary urgency loops are generated. Where pauses are interpreted as risk signals, urgency multiplies through reaction. The same workload can produce different stress textures depending on this interpretive norm.

As these norms repeat, legitimacy becomes less a personal achievement and more an environmental property. Participants entering the system inherit either a compressed pattern or a proportionate pattern, then reinforce it through ordinary interaction. No singular event establishes the pattern, and no singular event is required for it to persist.

System-level observation also suggests that restored legitimacy of judgment changes failure interpretation before it changes workload. In compressed environments, minor misses are often read as signs that people are not trying hard enough or not moving fast enough. In environments where judgment has standing, similar misses are more often read as information about fit, sequencing, or bandwidth constraints that can be mapped without immediate escalation. This shift does not remove accountability. It redistributes where accountability is applied: less on symbolic urgency performance, more on proportional response quality over repeated cycles. The practical effect is often subtle. Teams still run tight schedules, still handle interruptions, and still make tradeoffs under pressure. What changes is the threshold for converting every variance into a system-wide alarm. Over time, this threshold adjustment can reduce secondary turbulence that previously came from interpretation cascades rather than from the original event. Time-delayed recognition is common because participants first notice less noise, not more clarity. They may describe a period as simply calmer, then later see that calmness persisted even when demand levels rose again.

Retrospective comparison then reveals that legitimacy of judgment had become embedded in process behavior: fewer reflexive over-commitments, more explicit uncertainty boundaries, and less need to demonstrate commitment through pace alone. None of this requires a manifesto. It is carried through repeated everyday exchanges in which evaluation is treated as part of work rather than as an interruption to work.

In that sense, legitimacy is observed less in statements and more in repeated handling of ordinary pressure. The same incoming demands are met, but fewer of them are allowed to define the total frame. Small delays are processed without immediate inflation, and mixed signals are held without automatic narrative closure. Over time, this repeated proportioning becomes part of the system's default behavior rather than a temporary response style.

Over longer intervals, this yields an environment where judgment participation is ordinary enough to be unnoticed in daily operations, yet visible in comparative hindsight through reduced interpretive turbulence around similar classes of demand.

In repeated practice, this produces steadier interpretation of ordinary variance, with less automatic inflation and less dependence on urgency as proof of seriousness.

Over repeated intervals, this keeps judgment integrated with execution instead of forcing it into post-hoc correction only.

The same proportional handling can persist without fanfare as part of normal operations under recurring pressure.

It becomes visible mainly through repeated low-noise responses to recurring demand patterns.

Viewed longitudinally, legitimacy stays embedded through repetition rather than declaration: recurring demands arrive, proportional interpretation holds, and fewer cycles escalate into system-wide urgency language. The result is a durable low-noise response pattern that persists across ordinary pressure changes.

This continuation remains observable in routine cycles.

Over time, that repeated handling keeps interpretive pressure proportionate.

Chapter 15

When Nothing Changes, but Everything Has Shifted

After judgment returns, many people look around and feel confused.

Nothing seems different.

The work still exists. The obligations remain. The structure has not collapsed.

This lack of visible change can feel disappointing. People expect insight to produce movement. They anticipate a clear next step.

When that step does not appear, they question the value of what has shifted.

In reality, the most significant change is often positional.

Before, you were inside the system, responding from within its momentum. Now, you are slightly offset.

The system continues, but it no longer speaks with your voice.

This offset is subtle. It does not announce itself. It is felt as distance rather than decision.

Distance creates perspective. Perspective does not alter facts, but it alters relation.

You are still present, but not fused.

This difference matters even if nothing external moves.

Previously, demands passed directly into action. Now, they pause.

That pause is small, but consistent.

It creates a gap between stimulus and response. In that gap, judgment lives.

Because the gap is internal, others may not notice it. They see continuity. They assume sameness.

This assumption can be unsettling. You feel different, but the world reflects nothing back.

This mismatch can create doubt. People wonder if the change is real or imagined.

It is real.

Structural shifts often occur before outcomes register.

Think of alignment rather than transformation. Alignment does not produce spectacle. It produces stability.

Stability is quiet.

Quiet changes are easy to overlook because they do not demand attention. They do not disrupt routine.

But they accumulate.

The internal gap widens gradually. Responses become more deliberate. Reactions soften.

You may notice that situations which once triggered urgency now feel tolerable.

This tolerance is not indifference. It is proportion.

Proportion allows choice without pressure.

Importantly, this change does not require withdrawal. You can remain engaged without being absorbed.

Engagement without absorption feels unfamiliar.

Many people mistake it for detachment. They worry they are losing interest or becoming disengaged.

What they are losing is compulsion.

Compulsion kept them moving even when clarity was absent. Without it, movement slows.

Slowing does not mean stopping. It means recalibration.

Recalibration takes time. It rarely produces immediate results.

Because of this, people often underestimate its significance. They focus on what has not changed.

They miss what has.

The absence of urgency. The reduction of noise. The return of perspective.

These shifts alter how future decisions will be made, even if no decision has been made yet.

The system may continue unchanged for some time.

That is not failure. It is transition.

Transitions that are internal do not follow deadlines.

They unfold unevenly. They test patience.

During this period, people are tempted to force an outcome to validate the change.

They seek confirmation. They want proof.

Proof arrives later, often indirectly.

It shows up in how situations are handled. In what no longer feels necessary. In what can now be questioned.

These are not dramatic moments. They are quiet recognitions.

Over time, the accumulation becomes clear.

You are no longer carried. You are standing.

Standing does not require movement. It requires balance.

Balance feels different from momentum. It does not pull forward. It holds.

From this position, future action will be different, not because you decided something, but because you are deciding from else-where.

That elsewhere is the shift.

It does not need to announce itself to be real.

Nothing may have changed, but the way change will happen has already been altered.

That alteration is enough.

One recurring scene unfolds in the same office, at the same desk, with the same sequence of morning tasks. Screens open, messages are reviewed, and recurring obligations move across the day as before. From the outside, continuity is complete. Internally, a small offset is present. The person notices that familiar requests no longer pass directly into automatic agreement. A brief pause appears before response. The pause is subtle and often invisible. Yet it marks a shift in relation, not in workload.

In this phase, visible sameness can create doubt. People expect significant inner change to produce visible rearrangement. When re-arrangement does not appear, they question whether anything shifted at all. The doubt is understandable because social feedback is min-imal. Others continue interacting as if nothing has changed, and the unchanged interaction mirrors back an image of continuity. The person experiences discontinuity without confirmation, which can feel unstable even when orientation has become clearer.

A similar pattern appears in family routines. Meals happen at usual times, logistics are coordinated, and conversations follow familiar topics. The person who has shifted internally still partici-pates, still contributes, still keeps commitments. What changes is the degree of fusion with collective momentum. Certain tensions that once triggered immediate intervention are now observed first. Not every gap is filled instantly. The household remains functional, and the external picture remains largely unchanged, while inner posture becomes less compulsive.

Temporal delay is central because internal repositioning often precedes external consequence by long intervals. A changed stance may alter micro-responses today, then accumulate into different outcomes weeks later. In the meantime, the system appears stable. Without visible indicators, people are tempted to force external change to validate internal movement. Forcing can create spectacle, but spectacle is not required for real shift. Many shifts become consequential through repeated low-amplitude differences rather than single visible decisions.

In team settings, this may look like continued participation with altered emphasis. A person still attends planning meetings yet asks narrower questions, avoids broad commitments, and leaves certain assumptions unreinforced. The agenda remains unchanged. The meeting ends on schedule. Observers may report business as usual. Underneath, the contribution pattern has changed enough to alter future conversations incrementally. The alteration is difficult to detect in one session and easier to detect across months.

Hesitation before naming the shift often persists because language tends to oversimplify. Saying "everything changed" feels inaccurate when daily structures remain intact. Saying "nothing changed" also feels inaccurate because the internal relationship to those structures has moved. People oscillate between these incomplete descriptions. The oscillation delays articulation and keeps the shift private. Private shifts can still be real. They simply lack immediate shared vocabulary.

Another recurring scene appears in moments of urgency. Previously, urgency translated directly into accelerated action. Now urgency encounters an internal checkpoint. The person still acts, sometimes quickly, but not with the same automatic absorption. They can feel urgency without becoming identical to it. Externally, this may register only as slightly different tone or timing. Internally, it registers as a widening gap between signal and identification. The gap is the shift, even when no overt decision follows.

Because nothing obvious changes, others may continue assigning old narratives to the person. They are still seen as the stabilizer, the rapid responder, the one who carries difficult intervals. The person may continue fulfilling parts of these narratives while no longer fully inhabiting them. This partial participation can feel ambiguous. It is neither rejection nor endorsement. It is continuation under altered relation, with boundaries forming gradually rather than through explicit declaration.

In personal projects, the same structure appears when someone continues working on familiar material while no longer treating it as core identity. Output may remain steady. The emotional charge around output declines. Success and setback still matter, but their interpretive weight changes. Outsiders notice continuity of production and infer continuity of attachment. The inference misses the internal repositioning that now governs how effort is interpreted and how much of the self is invested in each cycle.

The delay between position and consequence can be disorienting. A person may feel fundamentally reoriented yet see no immediate change in obligations, opportunities, or social response. This gap invites skepticism about the shift's significance. Over time, significance appears indirectly: fewer reflexive commitments, slower escalation in conflict, reduced need to maintain appearances, and altered tolerance for unclear demands. None of these changes requires dramatic announcement. They emerge through repeated small deviations from prior compulsion.

Scene repetition reinforces the pattern. Monday looks like last Monday. Weekly reviews resemble prior reviews. Familiar conversations recur. Within this repetition, tiny differences persist: one less automatic promise, one more clarifying question, one silence where immediate reassurance used to appear. These differences do not transform the structure overnight. They accumulate as micro-adjustments that gradually reshape how the person occupies unchanged environments.

In institutions, unchanged appearance can even be strategically useful. Visible disruption invites interpretation and reaction from systems that prefer continuity. Internal repositioning allows a person to maintain participation while reducing involuntary reinforcement of patterns they no longer endorse fully. This does not resolve structural tension. It creates room for perception to remain active without immediate confrontation. The room can be narrow, but it is still distinct from total absorption.

During this period, judgment is often provisional. The person sees more clearly than before and still refrains from final declarations about meaning or direction. Provisional judgment can feel unsatisfying because it lacks closure. Yet closure is not always available at the pace expected by external rhythms. Daily life continues requiring response. The person responds while keeping interpretation open, allowing further evidence to accumulate before translating internal shift into larger visible moves.

Across contexts, the repeated geometry remains: external form persists, internal relation loosens, and consequential differences unfold below the threshold of immediate visibility. The process does not produce a climax. It produces duration. Over duration, unchanged scenes are inhabited differently, and that difference gradually alters future possibilities without requiring a single definitive turning point.

The chapter remains unresolved in ordinary time. People continue attending meetings, managing households, honoring commitments, and moving through familiar settings. At the same time, they do so from a changed position that is not easily legible to others. Nothing appears transformed, yet the basis of participation has shifted, and the effects of that shift continue to accumulate quietly.

No final signal confirms completion. The inner offset remains present, sometimes stronger, sometimes faint, while external routines proceed. The world reports sameness. The person experiences altered relation inside that sameness. Both descriptions remain true at once, and the period continues without a singular conclusion.

When external form remains unchanged, people often look for confirmation in subtle sensory cues rather than events. A meeting that once felt absorbing now feels slightly distant. A routine request that once triggered urgency now feels negotiable. A familiar conflict that once occupied the whole day now recedes faster. These cues are easy to discount because they are subjective and uneven. Their repetition over time, however, can indicate that positional change is real even without visible structural movement.

In organizations, unchanged dashboards can mask changed participation. Metrics may remain stable while individuals alter how much compensatory labor they contribute behind the metrics. For a period, outputs look identical. The internal distribution of effort is different. If compensatory labor decreases gradually, effects may appear only after delays and be attributed to unrelated factors. During the delay, observers conclude that nothing has shifted, while shifts are already underway at the level of role occupancy.

Another repeated scene is social mirroring. Others continue reflecting the older version of a person because social memory lags personal repositioning. Invitations, assumptions, and requests target the old pattern. The person may comply partially while feeling less identified with the role being projected. This partial compliance sustains external sameness and prolongs the period where internal and external descriptions diverge.

Hesitation before naming the shift is reinforced by this divergence. Naming too early can seem overstated when external evidence is sparse. Naming too late can allow old narratives to harden further. People often stay in intermediate language: something is different, nothing is settled, routine continues. Intermediate language can sound vague, yet it may be the most accurate description available while consequences are still incubating.

In personal projects, unchanged output can coexist with changed meaning. A person continues producing at similar volume while experiencing reduced attachment to recognition cycles that once drove pacing. The change may not alter deliverables immediately. It alters interpretation of those deliverables and willingness to distort priorities for external validation. Over time, this interpretive shift can influence decisions. In early phases, it remains mostly invisible.

Across contexts, repeated non-events matter. No dramatic confrontation occurs. No immediate reorganization appears. Still, the person occupies the same scenes with a different center of gravity. The difference accumulates through tiny decisions that preserve continuity while reducing compulsion. Continuity and shift coexist without resolution.

The period remains structurally quiet. Calendars stay full, obligations remain active, and relationships continue in familiar patterns. Beneath that quiet, position keeps changing incrementally. External confirmation may arrive later, partially, or not at all. The absence of confirmation does not eliminate the shift; it leaves it in prolonged coexistence with visible sameness.

Sometimes the only visible evidence of shift is that familiar scenes no longer consume the same amount of inner bandwidth. The person still attends, responds, and participates, yet less of the self is organized around maintaining older momentum. This evidence is subtle and often private, which is why external narratives of sameness can persist for long intervals.

Across time, these low-visibility changes may eventually alter outward patterns, but during the transition the dominant experience is coexistence: unchanged form, changed relation, and no singular event to confirm either.

Because the shift is positional, it may never produce a single event that marks completion. External routines can continue almost unchanged while internal relation keeps evolving by degree. In that condition, certainty about what has changed arrives slowly, through repeated small differences rather than visible rupture.

The person remains in familiar scenes, and familiar scenes remain in place, while the basis of participation continues to move beneath the surface of ordinary time.

In that prolonged interval, unchanged scenes continue to host changed participation, and recognition of the shift arrives, if at all, through gradual accumulation rather than immediate display.

The continuation of this state is not dramatic: same locations, same obligations, different internal relation repeated over time. That repetition itself becomes the scene, with change occurring in degree rather than event.

Chapter 16

When Judgment No Longer Needs to Resolve

Once judgment has returned and pressure has eased, a new expectation often appears.

People assume that clarity must eventually resolve into a decision.

They wait for the moment when everything lines up and an obvious move presents itself.

When this moment does not arrive, they grow uneasy. They wonder if judgment is incomplete.

In reality, judgment does not always resolve. Sometimes it stabilizes.

Stability is different from conclusion. A conclusion closes. Stability holds.

Holding can feel unsatisfying in cultures that prize outcomes. We are taught to finish, to decide, to move on.

Judgment resists this demand. It does not aim to end uncertainty. It aims to place it correctly.

When uncertainty is placed correctly, it stops dominating attention. It becomes background rather than foreground.

This shift is subtle. Questions remain, but they no longer press for answers.

The absence of pressure is often mistaken for stagnation. People fear they are stuck because nothing is pushing them forward.

But being pushed is not the same as being oriented.

Orientation provides a sense of where you are without telling you where to go. It allows you to see options without selecting one.

This ability is rare because it requires restraint.

Restraint means allowing situations to exist without intervention. It means tolerating incomplete narratives.

Many people have never experienced this. They move from confusion to action, from action to exhaustion, without resting in orientation.

When orientation appears, it feels unfamiliar.

There is no urgency. No compulsion. No justification needed.

This absence can be disconcerting. People look for signals. They wait for motivation, for desire, for certainty.

When none arrive, they worry that judgment has failed.

But judgment is not meant to motivate. It is meant to situate.

Once situated, action regains proportion. It no longer needs to justify existence. It can wait.

Waiting here is not avoidance. It is alignment maintained.

Alignment does not demand motion. It demands coherence.

Coherence exists when perception, tolerance, and response are not at odds.

From this position, doing nothing does not feel like loss. It feels neutral.

Neutrality is powerful. It removes the bias toward continuation. It removes the bias toward disruption.

Both options can now be seen without distortion.

This does not make choice easier. It makes it cleaner.

A clean choice does not rush. It does not perform. It does not seek validation.

It emerges when conditions align, or it does not emerge at all.

Judgment does not need to force it.

Many people fear that without pressure, they will drift.

Drift occurs when orientation is absent, not when it is present.

Orientation anchors. It allows movement when movement makes sense, and stillness when it does not.

Stillness is not inertia. It is readiness without demand.

This readiness changes how future events will be met. Responses will be less reactive. Commitments will be entered differently.

Not because rules were learned, but because position has shifted.

Judgment that does not resolve is not unfinished. It is complete in a different way.

It has done what it needed to do: it has restored proportion.

From here, nothing needs to be decided for the state to remain valid.

Judgment can stay.

From a system-level perspective, unresolved judgment often functions as a stable operating condition rather than a temporary failure to decide. Teams, families, and individuals can continue coordinated activity while holding open questions at low intensity in the background. The absence of closure does not automatically block movement. It changes the relation between movement and certainty. Movement proceeds with narrower claims and less demand that every action represent a final position.

In environments that value outcomes, this condition is easy to misread as drift. Longitudinal observation often shows something quieter: repeated orientation without forced convergence. People revisit the same structural question at intervals, each time with slightly different context, and each time without collapsing it into definitive resolution. The repetition is not circular in a dramatic sense. It is periodic recalibration under changing conditions.

Time-delayed recognition appears when participants later notice that many problematic escalations were avoided not by decisive intervention, but by sustained non-compulsive handling of ambiguity. Work kept moving, relationships stayed functional, and no singular turning point explains why. What changed was tolerance for unresolved states. This tolerance reduced pressure to overcommit early explanations and reduced the need for corrective reversals later.

At structural distance, one can see that resolution pressure and orientation pressure are different forces. Resolution pressure seeks endpoint legibility. Orientation pressure seeks accurate positioning in ongoing time. Systems can privilege one or the other. Where orientation pressure is allowed, unresolved judgment can remain coherent for long stretches without becoming chaotic. Where only endpoint legibility is recognized, the same condition may be mislabeled as indecision.

Quiet repetition makes the distinction visible. Similar situations recur, and responses are proportionate without pretending finality. Questions remain present but stop dominating local execution. Participants continue making bounded commitments while leaving frame-level interpretation open. This pattern does not produce a narrative climax. It produces continuity under uncertainty that is carried, observed, and periodically re-situated.

The chapter remains in that carried state. Judgment stays active, closure stays optional, and the system keeps operating with a form of steadiness that does not depend on decisive conclusion.

A system-level reading also shows how unresolved judgment can support temporal flexibility in coordination. When actors do not force immediate closure, they can keep commitments bounded and revisable as new information appears. This reduces abrupt reversals that often follow premature certainty. The tradeoff is that shared narratives remain less definitive for longer periods. In some environments, this is experienced as lack of closure. In others, it is experienced as reduced volatility.

Across institutions, recurring non-resolution is often managed through cadence rather than decision points. Teams revisit frame questions on regular intervals while continuing routine operations between intervals. The revisits are modest and do not always produce directional shifts. Their value lies in maintaining contact with orientation without turning every review into a referendum. Over time, this cadence can normalize the idea that coherence is maintained through periodic re-situating, not one-time final determination.

Time-delayed recognition appears when participants compare periods with forced decisions against periods with sustained orientation. Forced-decision periods can produce quick clarity followed by corrective work. Orientation periods can produce slower clarity with fewer large corrections. Neither pattern is universally superior, but the contrast becomes visible only across multiple cycles. Within any single cycle, unresolved judgment may still fccl likc an absence rather than an operating method.

From structural distance, the key repetition is simple. Questions arise, bounded action proceeds, questions remain partially open, context changes, questions are revisited. The loop is not a failure loop unless the surrounding system demands terminal answers for every frame issue. Many systems can function effectively in this loop, provided local commitments remain explicit and proportionate.

Quietly, this repeated loop changes expectations about what "complete" means in judgment-heavy environments. Completion can refer to current positioning rather than final resolution. Work can proceed from that positioning while interpretation continues evolving at a slower rate than day-to-day execution.

The chapter remains in that ongoing mode: unresolved where resolution is unnecessary, active where action is bounded, and continuously reoriented as conditions shift without requiring a dramatic endpoint.

Longitudinal observation also shows that unresolved judgment changes the type of commitment that gets made. Commitments tend to be narrower, time-bounded, and less interpretively loaded. This can lower the cost of revision because revisions are expected as context shifts. In systems that equate commitment with finality, such bounded commitments may look tentative. In systems that operate under variability, they can function as a stable adaptation pattern.

Delayed recognition appears when participants compare correction workload across periods. Periods driven by fast closure often produce clearer short-term narratives and heavier later rework when assumptions change. Periods that allow unresolved orientation often produce less narrative certainty and smaller correction spikes. Neither period is free of cost. The cost profile differs in timing and visibility.

From structural distance, this is a pacing issue rather than a motivational issue. Judgment that does not resolve is still governing proportion; it is just not producing terminal statements at every decision point. The system keeps moving through repeated cycles where action is bounded and interpretation remains revisable.

From distance, unresolved judgment also appears as a continuity strategy in systems that operate under nontrivial uncertainty but low immediate crisis. Such systems often gain more from preserving revisability than from extracting early definitive narratives. Participants can continue making concrete commitments, but those commitments are scoped so they do not require a total interpretation of the entire situation. This pattern is sometimes mistaken for indecision because public language around it is less dramatic and less final. Yet over repeated cycles it can produce stable behavior: fewer all-or-nothing swings, fewer identity-level declarations tied to temporary conditions, and fewer large corrections driven by overconfident early framing. Time-delayed recognition appears when people compare not only what was decided, but how costly later revisions became. Periods with forced closure may look decisive in real time and expensive in maintenance. Periods with unresolved orientation may look ambiguous in real time and less expensive in maintenance. The contrast is not universal, and it rarely appears inside a single week. It emerges through cumulative review of many ordinary intervals where action proceeded without requiring final interpretive closure. At structural scale, this is a governance pattern about how uncertainty is carried in motion. Uncertainty can be forced into statement, or it can be held in calibrated form while bounded actions continue. When held in calibrated form, judgment remains active as an orienting process rather than an endpoint-producing device. The system keeps moving, and coherence is maintained through periodic repositioning rather than terminal conclusions.

Seen across longer horizons, this also alters how systems interpret stability. Stability no longer means that every major question has a final answer. It means that action, review, and revision can coexist without producing constant crisis signals. Participants continue to navigate uncertainty, but uncertainty is carried as an ongoing variable rather than treated as an immediate defect to eliminate. This can look slow from close range and coherent from far range, especially when compared across multiple cycles where bounded action continues and frame interpretations keep updating.

This makes the system's continuity less dependent on decisive declarations and more dependent on repeated calibration. Actors continue to update local commitments as information changes, while preserving enough interpretive openness to avoid locking temporary conditions into permanent meaning. The resulting pattern is neither static nor dramatic; it is iterative, with coherence maintained through pacing rather than closure.

Across many cycles, participants can therefore remain highly active without pretending that all frame questions have reached endpoint form. Activity continues, uncertainty remains calibrated, and revision stays available without turning each revision into a crisis narrative.

In this configuration, coherence is maintained through repeated orientation checks embedded in routine work, not through one-time interpretive closure. The system remains active, revisable, and proportionate across changing conditions.

In repeated practice, this keeps adjustment costs distributed across time rather than concentrated at forced decision points.

This keeps practical motion continuous while interpretive closure remains intentionally deferred.

In practical terms, this means teams can continue committing, reviewing, and adapting while leaving some frame questions open without immediate interpretive penalty. Over time, that repeated stance functions as stable governance under uncertainty rather than as an absence of direction.

The pattern persists as ongoing calibration within ordinary execution.

This ongoing calibration allows uncertainty to be carried without forcing premature endpoint claims in every cycle.

That posture remains active across routine intervals.

It continues to shape coordination without requiring terminal interpretation.

It remains present as a repeated structural pattern across ongoing cycles.

This remains observable over time.

Chapter 17

When the World Does Not Respond

After judgment stabilizes, many people expect the outside world to shift.

They assume that once they see clearly, circumstances will follow. Opportunities will appear. Obligations will loosen. Something will open.

When this does not happen, disappointment sets in.

Nothing resists them explicitly. Nothing blocks them. Yet nothing responds.

This silence can feel unsettling. It creates the impression that judgment has led nowhere.

In reality, judgment does not negotiate with the world. It does not announce itself. It does not demand recognition.

The world responds to action, not to orientation.

This mismatch creates confusion. People feel aligned internally, but unchanged externally.

They begin to doubt the value of alignment. They wonder if clarity was premature or irrelevant.

This doubt is understandable. We are accustomed to feedback. Effort produces results. Decisions produce consequences.

Judgment produces position.

Position is invisible. It does not alter schedules. It does not rewrite expectations. It does not cancel commitments.

At least not immediately.

This delay does not invalidate judgment. It simply reveals how much of life is structured around inertia.

Structures persist until acted upon. They do not dissolve because perspective changes.

Many people misinterpret this persistence as resistance. They believe the world is pushing back.

In most cases, the world is not pushing at all. It is continuing.

Continuation requires no endorsement. It proceeds by default.

When judgment returns, it does not interrupt continuation. It reframes it.

Reframing takes time to translate into form.

During this time, people experience a strange duality. They are less pressured, yet still constrained. More aware, yet still embedded.

This duality is uncomfortable because it defies expectation. We are taught that insight leads to change.

Sometimes it does. Often it does not.

Insight changes how change will occur, not whether it occurs immediately.

This distinction matters. Without it, people feel cheated by clarity. They expect payoff.

Payoff is a transactional idea. Judgment is not transactional.

Judgment does not guarantee improvement. It guarantees accuracy.

Accuracy can coexist with difficulty. It can coexist with limitation. It can coexist with waiting.

Waiting here is not passive. It is calibrated.

Calibration means recognizing what cannot be moved yet without reverting to pressure.

Many people rush this phase. They act to force response. They seek confirmation that alignment matters.

This action often recreates old dynamics. Urgency returns. Pressure rebuilds. Judgment recedes.

Understanding the lag between internal shift and external response prevents this regression.

It allows alignment to deepen without being tested prematurely.

The world will eventually respond, but not to clarity itself. It responds to changed behavior, to different boundaries, to altered commitments.

Those changes emerge gradually when judgment is allowed to remain primary.

For now, the absence of response is not failure. It is neutrality.

Neutrality is rare. It is the state where nothing is demanded and nothing is granted.

In neutrality, judgment is not challenged. It is simply unacknowledged.

This can feel lonely. No signal confirms correctness. No outcome validates position.

Yet this solitude is temporary. It marks the separation between orientation and consequence.

Consequence arrives later, often quietly.

People look back and realize that things changed not because they pushed, but because they stopped compensating.

That stopping is not an act. It is an absence.

The world notices absence more slowly than effort.

Until then, nothing may seem to happen.

That nothing is not emptiness. It is space holding.

Judgment does not need response to remain real.

It only needs to remain present long enough for the world to catch up.

A common scene follows an internal shift that receives no external acknowledgment. The person has adjusted orientation, sees patterns with more precision, and expects at least minor environmental response. Instead, routine proceeds unchanged. Emails arrive at usual cadence, responsibilities remain assigned as before, and social expectations continue at the same level. No one resists explicitly. No one adapts explicitly. The absence of reaction can feel like a signal, though its meaning is unclear.

In organizational life, this looks like unchanged demand curves after someone stops overcompensating internally. External stakeholders still send requests according to previous assumptions. Timelines are proposed with the same confidence. Meetings still allocate work to the same nodes. The system is not responding to internal clarity because internal clarity is not directly observable. Observable behavior may have shifted only slightly so far. The gap between orientation and visible consequence remains wide.

A similar pattern appears in households when one member recognizes limits but daily logistics continue in established form. The recognition does not automatically reassign chores, alter schedules, or reduce implicit coordination burdens. Others continue according to existing rhythm because existing rhythm remains legible. The person who shifted may feel both clearer and unrecognized. Nothing has contradicted the new judgment, yet nothing has reorganized around it either. The environment remains neutral, which can be interpreted as indifference.

Temporal delay is often underestimated. People expect systems to register changed posture quickly. Many systems register only changed outputs over repeated intervals. If output changes are incremental, recognition is incremental. During this lag, old assumptions keep operating. The person may wonder whether internal change has practical relevance. That doubt grows when days pass without visible adjustment. Still, lag alone does not invalidate orientation. It describes transmission speed between internal position and shared structure.

In professional teams, world non-response can be reinforced by politeness. Colleagues may sense subtle differences but avoid interpreting them publicly. Work continues through established channels. Because no explicit friction appears, everyone assumes continuity is preferred. This assumption preserves short-term smoothness. It also delays renegotiation. The team can remain in this state for months: internally shifting individuals operating inside externally stable expectations, with neither side fully naming the mismatch.

Hesitation before judgment takes a specific form here. A person asks whether the absence of response means the judgment was overstated or whether response simply has not arrived yet. Both possibilities remain plausible for a long period. Premature conclusions feel risky in either direction. Declaring the shift irrelevant could erase real perception. Declaring external resistance could project intent where there is only inertia. The uncertainty encourages continued observation without definitive interpretation.

Scene repetition makes the delay tangible. Week after week, the same requests arrive, the same routines reappear, and the same assumptions are re-enacted. The person responds with slightly different pacing or scope, but the broader pattern remains. Differences are too small to trigger immediate structural adaptation. Adaptation mechanisms in the environment are slow and often threshold-based. Until thresholds are crossed repeatedly, the world keeps presenting previous defaults.

In service relationships, clients may continue asking for expansive availability after boundaries have shifted internally. They ask this way not because they reject limits, but because prior behavior established a template. Templates persist until new patterns are observed consistently enough to replace them. During transition, each interaction can feel like evidence that nothing changed. In fact, each interaction may be part of the slow process through which changed patterns become legible to others.

Another recurring scene is private recalculation. The person reviews recent weeks and notices that external response remains muted. They measure subtle internal gains against visible external sameness. The comparison can feel discouraging because external confirmation is culturally treated as proof. Internal orientation lacks that proof. Yet orientation still shapes choices at low amplitude. Low-amplitude changes are harder to detect in real time and easier to detect across larger windows.

Social narratives can magnify disappointment. Many narratives imply that clarity should immediately unlock opportunity or reduce burden. When the world does not respond, people may infer that clarity failed. An alternative interpretation is that systems operate on delayed feedback and require repeated behavioral evidence before changing allocation patterns. This interpretation does not guarantee eventual response. It contextualizes why immediate response is not common, especially in environments optimized for continuity.

In institutions with high inertia, unchanged external response may continue even after repeated small adjustments. Governance cycles, contractual commitments, and reporting routines can absorb minor variation without visible adaptation. Individuals inside such systems may experience prolonged duality: altered internal stance combined with persistent external demand patterns. Duality becomes ordinary. Ordinary duality is difficult to explain because it lacks obvious events, consisting instead of accumulated non-events over time.

The repeated structure across contexts is straightforward: orientation shifts internally, external defaults persist, interpretation remains unsettled. No confrontation is required for this to happen. No antagonism is required. Continuation by default can fully explain the silence. Silence nevertheless carries psychological weight because humans look for reciprocal signals after meaningful internal change. When reciprocal signals do not appear, patience is tested and interpretation becomes more complex.

In friendships and communities, non-response can also reflect distributed attention rather than resistance. Others are managing their own momentum and may not perceive subtle shifts quickly. The person who changed remains visible in old role outlines for longer than expected. Invitations, requests, and assumptions keep matching historical patterns. The mismatch between current orientation and received expectations persists as a quiet friction that seldom produces overt conflict yet remains present in each exchange.

Across extended time, consequence often emerges through accumulation of small absences rather than dramatic acts. A person stops supplying certain forms of invisible stabilization. At first nothing visible changes. Later, minor frictions appear in places previously kept smooth. Even then, interpretation is delayed. Frictions are attributed to busyness, seasonality, or chance. The environment takes time to map new patterns. During mapping, the world still appears unresponsive even as adaptation has begun at low resolution.

This stage has no clear endpoint. Some contexts eventually reflect the internal shift; others remain largely unchanged for long periods. Meanwhile, daily life continues under mixed signals: accurate internal orientation, limited external acknowledgment, and slow emergence of indirect consequences. The person remains engaged with ordinary obligations while carrying an unresolved relation between clarity and response.

The scene remains open in neutral time. Messages continue, routines continue, and assumptions continue, even as participation gradually changes in texture. The world does not immediately answer internal judgment. It continues in its own tempo, and recognition, if it arrives, arrives later than expected.

World non-response is often most visible in administrative systems. Forms, queues, and scheduling logic continue processing requests according to prior categories. Internal orientation does not automatically create a new category, so the person keeps receiving the same prompts and obligations. The system is not rejecting the shift; it is simply operating on established inputs. Until inputs become consistently different in observable ways, outputs remain similar and response appears absent.

In collaborative work, this can manifest as unchanged expectations after someone internally reduces tolerance for overextension. Colleagues continue asking for rapid turnarounds because prior responsiveness set the baseline. Early attempts to slow pace may be interpreted as temporary overload rather than lasting repositioning. Requests continue, and the person experiences repeated mismatch between current orientation and inherited expectation. Mismatch alone does not force adaptation. Adaptation often requires repeated, legible divergence.

Another recurring scene is interpretive drift. Because external feedback is quiet, the person cycles through explanations: perhaps nothing changed internally, perhaps others have not noticed, perhaps notice occurred but no one knows how to respond. None of these explanations can be verified quickly. The cycle repeats after each ordinary day where routines persist. Ambiguity becomes part of the environment, and judgment continues under low-confirmation conditions.

Temporal delay can be extended by distributed systems where no single actor owns adjustment. Each participant responds locally and assumes someone else may initiate broader change. Without coordination, small shifts remain local. Local shifts are real but insufficient to alter the whole pattern quickly. The person who changed internally may therefore encounter long intervals of apparent non-response even as small adaptive signals begin appearing at edges.

In personal networks, old role assignments can persist through goodwill. Friends and relatives may continue leaning on familiar capacities because those capacities were reliable for years. Their reliance reflects trust and habit more than disregard. The person perceives continued demand without corresponding acknowledgment of changed position. Trust and mismatch coexist. Neither produces immediate resolution.

Across these scenes, the repeated structure is neutral and persistent: orientation changes, defaults continue, adaptation lags. The lag can feel empty because there is little narrative content in non-response. Yet non-response has structure. It reflects inertia, template persistence, and slow social updating rather than clear verdict on the value of internal judgment.

The chapter remains open in that lag. Daily exchanges continue with mixed signals, and consequences remain delayed. Over time, small differences may accumulate into visible response, or default patterns may continue longer than expected. In either case, the present period is defined by continuation of the world at its prior tempo while internal clarity remains active without immediate external reply.

Even when non-response continues, internal orientation can remain stable. The person keeps noticing where defaults persist and where small deviations begin to register. Some days look identical to before; other days show minor shifts in expectation or timing. The pattern is mixed and slow, with no clear threshold when world response can be declared present.

For long stretches, the practical reality is this unresolved lag: clarity on one side, continuation on the other, and gradual change unfolding below obvious visibility.

This lag can continue without signaling error. Systems often update at a slower pace than internal recognition, and social roles often persist longer than the perceptions that first sustained them. During that interval, silence from the world remains common and ambiguous.

The person continues operating within that ambiguity: clear enough internally to notice defaults, not yet met with a fully visible external response, and still moving through unchanged routines while consequences gather gradually.

Until then, the world's tempo and the person's revised orientation continue side by side, linked by delay rather than immediate reciprocity.

In that interval, non-response remains part of the structure rather than an exception to it. The world continues on prior defaults while internal clarity continues to register those defaults with increasing precision.

Chapter 18

Why Judgment Does Not Need to Be Explained

When judgment stabilizes, a new pressure often appears.

People feel the need to explain.

They want to justify their position. They want others to understand. They want coherence to be shared.

This impulse is natural. We are social. Meaning feels safer when it is recognized.

But explanation carries cost.

To explain is to translate judgment into terms that are acceptable, defensible, and complete.

Judgment is rarely any of these.

It is partial. It is evolving. It holds ambiguity.

Explanation compresses. It selects. It resolves.

When judgment is explained too early, it is reshaped to fit expectation. It becomes clearer to others, but less accurate to oneself.

This reshaping happens subtly. People emphasize reasons that sound reasonable. They omit hesitation. They simplify context.

In doing so, they trade fidelity for legibility.

Legibility is rewarded. Clear stories are easier to accept. Definitive statements inspire confidence.

Judgment does not inspire confidence. It inspires orientation.

Because of this mismatch, judgment often feels exposed when left unexplained.

Silence is misinterpreted. Others ask questions. They fill gaps with assumptions.

These reactions create pressure. People feel obligated to clarify, to reassure, to make things make sense.

This obligation can pull judgment back into performance. It becomes something to defend rather than something to hold.

Defense narrows perspective. It locks position. It discourages revision.

Once judgment is defended, changing it feels like retreat. People stick with explanations even when their understanding evolves.

This stickiness is dangerous. It hardens provisional insight into fixed stance.

Judgment thrives on revisability. It needs freedom to adjust as conditions change.

Explanation reduces that freedom.

This does not mean silence is superior. It means timing matters.

Judgment that is still settling benefits from privacy. Not secrecy, but protection.

Protection allows perception to deepen without being forced into narrative.

Many people fear that without explanation, they will appear evasive or irresponsible.

This fear is understandable. Silence can be misread.

But explanation is not the only alternative. Presence communicates. Consistency communicates. Boundaries communicate.

Judgment can be enacted without being articulated.

Others may not understand immediately. They may never understand fully.

Understanding is not required for judgment to remain valid.

The need to be understood often comes from insecurity, not from clarity.

Clarity is comfortable with delay. It does not rush recognition.

When judgment is secure, it does not seek agreement. It does not demand endorsement.

It remains open without becoming unstable.

This openness can feel lonely. Explanations create connection. Silence creates distance.

Distance is not disconnection. It is space without distortion.

In that space, judgment can breathe.

Over time, people notice that fewer explanations are needed. Not because others stopped asking, but because the need to answer softened.

Responses become simpler. Not defensive, not persuasive.

"I'm still thinking." "This is where I am right now." "I don't need to decide yet."

These statements do not resolve tension. They contain it.

Containment is powerful. It prevents escalation. It preserves integrity.

Judgment does not need to be explained to be legitimate.

It does not owe coherence to others before it has settled within.

Explanation can come later, when clarity has stabilized.

Until then, judgment is allowed to remain unspoken, held quietly, without apology.

That permission is part of what allows judgment to remain intact.

In system terms, explanation pressure tends to rise when surrounding actors need predictability more than nuance. Coordinators, peers, and stakeholders map behavior through stated reasons because reasons are easy to circulate. When judgment is still settling, available reasons are partial and sometimes unstable. This creates a recurring mismatch: the system requests finalized narrative while the underlying orientation remains provisional. The mismatch is not conflict by itself, but it creates steady translation load.

From observer distance, early explanation often appears as a synchronization tool rather than a truth tool. It aligns expectations quickly, lowers social uncertainty, and keeps coordination friction low. These are valid functions. Over longer windows, however, rapid synchronization can freeze language around interpretations that were only temporary. People then coordinate around those frozen statements even as lived understanding continues to evolve. Later revisions look inconsistent, though the deeper process was continuous.

Time-delayed recognition is common here. Participants may not notice distortion while explanation is solving immediate communication problems. Months later, they observe that defended explanations outlasted the conditions that generated them. Behavior shifted gradually, but shared narrative lagged behind. The lag produced avoidable confusion, not because anyone acted in bad faith, but because the system rewarded early legibility over ongoing fidelity.

At structural scale, one can see two different economies at work. Legibility economy values concise, stable accounts that can be distributed quickly. Fidelity economy values nuanced, revisable accounts that track changing context. Most environments tilt toward legibility economy under pressure. Individuals then feel compelled to convert living judgment into fixed statements earlier than accuracy permits. The conversion helps coordination now and increases reinterpretation work later.

Quiet repetition shows this clearly. Similar prompts for explanation recur, similar compressed answers are offered, similar private revisions occur afterward. Public language remains cleaner than internal understanding for extended periods. No single exchange causes the gap. The gap is produced by repeated, ordinary attempts to make complex orientation portable in fast-moving social systems.

The chapter remains open in that repeated gap. Judgment continues to evolve, explanation continues to be requested, and systems continue privileging what can be shared quickly even when what is most accurate is still in motion.

At a broader scale, explanation demand can be viewed as a co-ordination protocol. Systems ask for articulated reasons so multiple actors can align without direct access to one another's private context. This protocol works well for stable decisions. It works less well for evolving judgment that is still updating. When evolving judgment is forced into stable language, coordination improves in the short term while interpretive debt accumulates in the background.

Interpretive debt appears later as repeated clarification cycles. Participants revisit prior statements to add nuance, correct overreach, or detach old wording from new context. None of these revisions is unusual. What is notable is their frequency when early explanations were made under pressure. External observers often see the same sequence across projects: quick narrative compression, temporary alignment, later narrative repair. The sequence is operationally understandable and structurally costly.

Time-delayed recognition tends to happen in document trails. Early records show confident framing. Mid-period records show exceptions and caveats. Later records show broader reframing that absorbs those caveats. Teams reading the trail backward can see that judgment was moving throughout, even when outward language suggested fixity. The delay between movement and representation is where much of the friction is generated.

From system distance, this is not primarily a communication skill problem. It is a timing problem between two legitimate needs: portable explanation and faithful representation. Portable explanation needs short, stable forms. Faithful representation needs revisability and context. Under pressure, short stable forms dominate. Over time, context re-enters and short forms become insufficient. The cycle repeats as new pressure episodes arrive.

Quiet repetition stabilizes the cycle as normal practice. Requests for explanation continue, partial explanations continue, later refinements continue. Individuals can appear inconsistent while actually tracking changing conditions more accurately than their early summaries allowed. The mismatch is produced by protocol constraints as much as by personal choice.

The chapter remains active in that mismatch. Judgment continues evolving at one tempo, explanation continues being requested at another tempo, and systems continue coordinating around whichever form can travel fastest at the moment.

A final external observation concerns role differentiation inside explanation-heavy systems. Some actors specialize in producing fast, coherent accounts, while others specialize in holding contextual nuance until it can be represented safely. When these roles are not recognized, the second role can look like delay or ambiguity. When recognized, both roles are treated as necessary parts of coordination under uncertainty.

Time-delayed understanding usually arrives when systems review mismatches between declared rationale and later behavior. Instead of reading mismatch only as inconsistency, observers begin to see it as evidence that explanation and judgment were operating on different clocks. The declarations traveled quickly because they had to. The deeper orientation moved more slowly because context kept shifting.

Quiet repetition sustains this distinction. Explanation requests continue, concise answers continue, contextual updates continue, and the environment keeps balancing portability against fidelity without fully eliminating tension between them.

A system perspective also shows that explanation demand is unevenly distributed across roles and moments. In high-visibility moments, actors are asked for concise accounts that can travel quickly through organizational layers. In lower-visibility moments, the same actors continue updating their own orientation with additional context that cannot be compressed without distortion. This produces a recurring two-track reality: portable narrative for coordination, evolving understanding for local accuracy. Friction arises when one track is assumed to be a full substitute for the other. Delayed recognition often comes when teams revisit decisions that seemed fully explained at the time and find that many later adjustments were not reversals of principle but incorporations of context that was unavailable or inarticulable in the initial account. The mismatch then appears less like inconsistency and more like normal temporal layering of judgment and communication. At structural distance, the issue is not whether to explain, but when explanation hardens beyond the phase it was meant to serve. If it hardens too early, future nuance looks like backtracking. If it remains revisable, coordination may feel less certain in the short term. Most systems oscillate between these states under pressure. Quiet repetition keeps the oscillation active: brief explanations are produced, then amended, then reinterpreted as conditions shift, while social expectations keep preferring fixed stories that can be reused across contexts. The process continues without final settlement, because both needs remain present: actors need language that coordinates now, and they need judgment that can keep pace with changing reality later.

When repeated over time, this two-clock dynamic becomes part of normal operations. Teams learn to coordinate around provisional language while continuing to revise local understanding as new details emerge. Tension does not disappear; it becomes managed through cadence and role differentiation rather than through one-time explanatory closure. Explanation remains necessary, judgment remains in motion, and both continue to interact without fully collapsing into a single stable account.

In this repeated configuration, explanation and judgment remain coupled but non-identical: one serves immediate distribution across the system, the other serves ongoing alignment with changing context. Neither fully replaces the other, and the gap between them is managed over time through revision, clarification, and continued operational coordination.

This ongoing gap is not necessarily an error condition; it is often the expected result of coordinating complex work through simplified language while judgment continues updating beneath that language. Over time, repeated updates can narrow the gap without requiring a single conclusive explanation that freezes interpretation prematurely.

As long as both clocks remain active, explanation continues to coordinate immediate action while judgment continues to track evolving context across longer intervals.

This dual-tempo coordination pattern can continue stably while both explanation and judgment keep updating at different speeds.

The interval between those tempos remains a routine feature rather than a temporary anomaly.

As the cycle repeats, coordination remains possible without demanding perfect representational finality at every step. Explanation continues serving immediate alignment, while judgment continues updating against context that becomes visible only over longer intervals.

That interval remains active as part of normal coordination.

Coordination continues inside that difference in tempo, with explanation and judgment remaining linked but non-identical over time.

As conditions continue to shift, this dual-track process remains present in everyday coordination.

The process remains ongoing under ordinary system conditions.

That pattern stays active through repeated operational intervals.

It continues as a stable background condition.

It remains observable across repeated periods of routine coordination.

This remains structurally consistent.

Chapter 19

Why the Absence of Conclusion Is Complete

Many readers reach this point expecting a conclusion.

They look for a final statement. A synthesis. A sentence that closes the loop.

This expectation is reasonable. Most books are designed to resolve. They move toward an answer and deliver it.

When that answer does not arrive, discomfort appears.

People wonder if something is missing. They assume the work is unfinished.

But completion does not always take the form of conclusion.

Some processes stabilize without resolving. Some understandings mature without closing.

Judgment is one of them.

Judgment aims to place things correctly, not to end inquiry. It seeks proportion, not finality.

A conclusion compresses. It selects one direction and discards the rest.

Compression can be useful. It enables action. It creates decisiveness.

But it also removes alternatives. It locks perspective.

When the situation itself remains open, a forced conclusion misrepresents it.

The absence of conclusion is not hesitation. It is fidelity.

Fidelity to complexity. Fidelity to uncertainty that cannot be reduced without distortion.

Many people confuse closure with relief. They believe that once a conclusion is reached, tension will disappear.

In practice, conclusions often replace one tension with another. They demand commitment. They create new obligations.

Judgment that stabilizes without concluding avoids this substitution.

It allows tension to soften without being redirected.

This softening is subtle. It does not announce completion. It feels like quiet.

Quiet is easily mistaken for emptiness.

In fact, quiet is density without noise. It holds many possibilities without pushing any forward.

This holding is unfamiliar. We are taught to move on, to decide, to finish.

Not finishing feels irresponsible.

But responsibility depends on context. When action is required, decisions matter. When orientation is required, conclusions can mislead.

Judgment that remains open keeps orientation intact.

It does not prevent action. It delays foreclosure.

Foreclosure is the act of closing options. It creates certainty at the cost of accuracy.

In many situations, accuracy matters more than certainty.

This priority is rarely stated, but it is felt.

People who reach this state often notice a shift. They are less reactive. Less compelled to justify. Less eager to announce direction.

They may feel incomplete, but they no longer feel lost.

This distinction matters.

Being incomplete is tolerable. Being lost is exhausting.

The absence of conclusion signals that judgment is present, not that it has failed.

It means the work of seeing has been done, even if the work of deciding has not.

Deciding can happen later, or not at all.

Judgment does not insist.

Completion here is not an endpoint. It is a posture.

A posture that allows life to be met as it unfolds, rather than forced into narrative.

This posture is quiet. It attracts little attention. It offers no slogans.

But it is stable.

Nothing needs to be added for it to remain so.

The absence of conclusion is not a gap.

It is the shape of an understanding that refuses to simplify what has not simplified itself.

That refusal is what makes it complete.

The central judgment can be repeated without reducing its ambiguity. Absence of conclusion can be complete. Completion does not have to appear as closure. Completion does not have to appear as final synthesis. Completion does not have to appear as a single statement that removes all remaining tension.

This is not a rhetorical trick. It is a boundary against an inherited equation. Inherited equation: complete means concluded. Counter-anchor: complete can mean adequately placed, not finally closed. The difference is small in wording and large in implication.

Another phrasing: Conclusion is one form of ending. Completion is one form of sufficiency. Ending and sufficiency can overlap.

Ending and sufficiency can also separate. This chapter marks that separation without forcing it into rule.

The same thought can be rendered by negation. Absence of conclusion is not automatically lack. Absence of conclusion is not automatically indecision. Absence of conclusion is not automatically avoidance. Absence of conclusion can be fidelity to what does not simplify under pressure.

This is not an argument against conclusions in all contexts. Conclusions can be necessary. Conclusions can be precise. Conclusions can carry valid force. The judgment here is narrower. When the object remains open, forced closure can misstate the object.

Another boundary: This is not an endorsement of vagueness for its own sake. Vagueness obscures. The anchor is about unresolved precision, not vague indecision. Unresolved precision can remain exact about boundaries while declining false finality.

The statement can be rephrased through what it refuses. It refuses premature compression. It refuses narrative completion as a substitute for structural accuracy. It refuses to treat lingering openness as error when openness belongs to the thing itself.

This is not a refusal to think. It is a refusal to over-close. Thinking can continue without endpoint declaration. Thinking can mature without terminal sentence. Maturity here is not measured by decisiveness alone.

Another restatement: Conclusion resolves by selecting. Selection excludes by design. When exclusion distorts the field, conclusion may provide relief at the price of misfit. Absence of conclusion keeps more of the field intact. Keeping more of the field intact can be a form of completion.

This is not anti-form. The chapter still has form. It still has limits. It still has a defined proposition. The proposition is that defined proposition does not require final closure to be complete.

The same proposition can be said in temporal terms. Completion can occur at the level of current orientation. Conclusion suggests final orientation. Current orientation and final orientation are not identical. The first can be valid without claiming the second.

Another boundary against misreading. Absence of conclusion is not suspended panic. Absence of conclusion is not endless postponement as performance. Absence of conclusion can be stable non-foreclosure. Stable non-foreclosure has its own structure.

This does not remove uncertainty. It relocates uncertainty. Uncertainty stops being treated as a defect to erase. Uncertainty becomes part of the domain being held accurately. Holding is not collapse. Holding is a mode of completion when endpoint claims would exceed the available fidelity.

Another phrasing keeps the same axis. Complete does not always mean finished. Complete can mean proportionate. Complete can mean no further compression is needed to maintain integrity at this level. No further compression needed is different from no further change possible.

This is not an escape from consequence. Absence of conclusion does not erase consequence. Actions and interpretations continue.

What is refused is a finalizing statement that would pretend the field has ceased to move.

Another boundary: The claim is not that all closure is distortion. The claim is that closure can distort when demanded by expectation rather than by fit. Expectation often asks for endings. Fit may ask for sustained openness. The chapter stays with fit.

The judgment can be restated through pressure. Pressure asks for ending language. Ending language can produce immediate legibility. Immediate legibility can be mistaken for adequacy. Adequacy here is measured by faithfulness, not by speed of legibility.

This is not a hidden method. No sequence is offered. No template is implied. No procedure is encoded beneath the language. Only a repeated distinction is being protected from collapse.

That distinction again: Conclusion and completion are related, not identical. When they diverge, forcing identity can reduce accuracy. Allowing divergence can preserve accuracy at the expense of immediate reassurance. The chapter declines reassurance as criterion.

Another line of negation: Not unfinished because unresolved. Not unfinished because open. Not unfinished because non-final. Potentially complete because proportion is restored without false foreclosure.

This is not a claim about passivity. Non-conclusion does not imply non-engagement. A position can remain active while unclosed. Interpretation can remain awake while unfinalized. The absence of conclusion does not empty the field. It keeps the field from being reduced below its own complexity.

The thought can be phrased as an epistemic boundary. Knowledge can reach sufficiency without reaching closure. Sufficiency means enough for honest relation. Closure means no remainder worth holding. These are different thresholds. The chapter anchors the first without pretending the second.

Another boundary statement: This is not the celebration of endlessness. Endlessness can be evasive. The anchor is not endlessness. The anchor is refusal of false ending. False ending is ending language not matched to structural state.

The same judgment in quieter rhythm: What is complete here is not a final answer. What is complete here is the placement of terms. The terms are placed enough to prevent major misreading. Further closure is not required for this level of integrity.

This is not relativism. Not all readings are equal. Not all framings are compatible. Boundaries are present. The absence of conclusion does not dissolve boundaries. It preserves boundaries while declining terminal simplification.

Another re-statement through what remains. Remainder is not failure. Remainder can be accurate residue. A conclusion often removes remainder by declaration. Completion here keeps remainder visible because remainder belongs to the object.

This is not anti-decision rhetoric. Decisions may still occur. The chapter does not forbid decision. It distinguishes decision from imposed conceptual closure. Decision can happen within open understanding. Open understanding need not pretend it has become closed in order to remain valid.

Another boundary against moral reading. Absence of conclusion is not moral superiority. Conclusion is not moral inferiority. The distinction is structural, not ethical. The question is fit between form of ending and state of what is being held.

The judgment can be repeated as a minimal sentence. No conclusion can still be complete. Complete can mean non-distorting. Non-distorting can mean still open. Still open can mean structurally faithful.

This is not contradiction to be repaired. It is a paired term set that resists premature fusion. Conclusion is one tool. Completion is one state. Tool and state do not have to coincide in every context.

Another phrasing: Closure provides decisional compactness. Completion provides orientational adequacy. Compactness may be too small for some fields. Adequacy may require retaining unresolved dimensions. Retaining unresolved dimensions can still count as complete in orientational terms.

This does not settle everything. It does not need to. Settling everything would exceed the anchor. The anchor is sufficient when it prevents one central misinterpretation: that open-endedness automatically proves incompletion.

Another boundary: No synthesis slogan is being offered. No final doctrine is being declared. No closing imperative is being attached. The chapter remains at the level of definitional restraint.

Restraint here means not over-speaking the state. If the state is open, language remains open. If language remains open, the text can still be complete as text. Textual completeness does not require conceptual foreclosure.

The same proposition can be recast through pressure and release. Conclusion releases one kind of pressure by ending debate. Absence of conclusion releases another kind of pressure by refusing distortion. The chapter tracks the second release without demanding the first.

This is not a strategy for avoiding responsibility. Responsibility can include refusing inaccurate closure. Responsibility can include acknowledging what remains unresolved without dramatizing it. The absence of conclusion can be the responsible form when finality would be performative rather than true.

Another repetition without escalation: Complete is not always closed. Closed is not always complete. Open is not always unfinished. Unfinished is not always open. The terms are adjacent, not interchangeable.

The judgment can be restated through fidelity again. Fidelity can require leaving edges unsealed. Sealed edges can look neat while falsifying interior movement. Unsealed edges can look incomplete while preserving interior proportion. The chapter chooses proportion over neatness.

This is not anti-reader language. It does not deny expectation. Expectation for endings is normal. The anchor only states that expectation does not determine structural truth. Structural truth here may include non-concluding completion.

Another boundary against therapeutic closure. Relief may accompany conclusion. Relief may also accompany accurate non-conclusion. Neither relief pattern is used here as final test. Relief is decoupled from correctness in this chapter's logic.

The proposition can be stated almost mathematically. If conclusion would require excluding relevant unresolved terms, then conclusion decreases fidelity. If non-conclusion preserves those terms without collapsing coherence, then non-conclusion can satisfy completeness conditions for the present frame. No moral claim is needed for this relation.

This is not permanent suspension as universal rule. The chapter does not universalize. It defines a specific fit between open object and open closure form. Where object closes, closure can close. Where object remains open, closure may remain open without incompleteness.

Another re-statement in plain rhythm. Nothing essential is missing simply because no final sentence closes all paths. What is needed for this chapter is already present: terms, boundaries, proportion, and a refusal of distortion. That package can be complete without being conclusive.

This refusal remains quiet. It does not argue loudly against endings. It does not celebrate uncertainty. It simply withholds one move: pretending that finality has arrived where finality is not yet structurally earned.

Again, without adding method. No conclusion can be complete. Complete can remain open. Open can remain exact. Exact can remain unresolved. Unresolved can remain sufficient.

The chapter can rest there. Not closed in the conventional sense. Not lacking in the anchor sense. Present, bounded, and non-foreclosed. That is the form of completion being named.

And this naming stays incomplete by design. It keeps ambiguity from being translated into error. It keeps non-conclusion from being translated into absence. It keeps completion from being confined to closure alone.

The final boundary is the same as the first boundary. Absence of conclusion is not automatically a gap. In this frame, absence of conclusion is the fitting form of completion. No further simplification is required for that judgment to hold.

Another way to hold the anchor is through terms of representational fit. A conclusion can over-represent confidence. An absence of conclusion can under-represent confidence. Neither risk is solved by default. The chapter chooses the second risk where the first would distort more severely.

This is not anti-confidence language. Confidence can remain local and bounded. What is withheld is global finality that exceeds the structure being addressed. Bounded confidence is compatible with non-concluding completion.

The same judgment in slower sequence. First, terms are placed. Second, boundaries are drawn. Third, false closure is declined.

These three moves can constitute completion for this frame. A fourth move, final synthesis, is optional and can be distorting if forced.

Another boundary: No conclusion is not a blank ending. It is an ending without foreclosure. Ending without foreclosure can still be definitive about what is rejected. Here, what is rejected is the demand that completion must culminate in simplification.

This is not resistance to meaning. Meaning is present. Meaning is distributed rather than compressed. Distributed meaning can feel less decisive while remaining more proportionate.

Another restatement in concise terms. Completion here equals adequate orientation plus intact ambiguity. Conclusion would reduce ambiguity. Reduction is not mandatory when ambiguity is structurally relevant.

This does not make ambiguity sacred. Ambiguity can be noise. Ambiguity can also be signal. The chapter leaves this distinction open while refusing blanket elimination.

Another boundary against performative openness. The text does not multiply uncertainty for effect. It keeps uncertainty where uncertainty already belongs. That retention is restraint, not inflation.

Again through negation. Not inconclusive because weak. Not inconclusive because evasive. Not inconclusive because unfinished labor. Potentially non-conclusive because concluding would misstate proportions.

The judgment can be reframed around lexical pressure. Words like final, ultimate, and definitive carry closure expectations. This chapter intentionally underuses that register. Underuse is structural, not stylistic ornament. It keeps language from claiming more closure than the domain supports.

Another restatement: The absence of conclusion can be complete when the task is anchoring, not ending. Anchoring secures interpretive boundaries. Ending secures narrative closure. These tasks can separate. Here they separate.

This is not refusal of readers. It is refusal of over-claim. Over-claim would present finished certainty where only positioned sufficiency exists. Positioned sufficiency is enough for this frame.

Another boundary statement: No prescriptive translation is attached. No practical lesson is extracted. No moral hierarchy is declared. The chapter remains where it began: in definitional distance.

The same line once more. Absence of conclusion is complete. Complete means the judgment is properly bounded. Complete does not mean ambiguity is erased. Complete does not mean all residual tension is removed. Complete means no further closure is required to avoid misreading the core terms.

This can remain unfinished in appearance and complete in function. Function here is interpretive fidelity. Fidelity has been maintained. Therefore completeness, in this sense, remains intact without concluding closure.

Another formulation protects the same boundary. Completion here is measured by adequacy of placement, not by terminal statement. Adequacy can be reached while openness remains. Openness can remain while coherence remains. Coherence can remain without a final sentence that closes all remainder.

This is not an unresolved defect. It is a resolved refusal of over-resolution. The distinction matters because over-resolution creates a false sense of finish. False finish is still distortion, even when it feels satisfying.

The chapter therefore keeps its shape. No conclusion is added as proof of completion. Completion is already present in the maintained proportion between what is defined and what is left rightly unsealed. The absence of conclusion remains complete in exactly that sense.

The same judgment can be repeated through a final set of non-equivalences. Open does not equal absent. Unclosed does not equal unworked. Non-final does not equal incoherent. Complete does not equal terminal. These pairs are often treated as interchangeable. This chapter keeps them separated.

Separation here is not stylistic complexity. It is protective precision. When these terms collapse into each other, readers are pushed toward one false inference: if no final conclusion appears, the work remains incomplete. The anchor has spent its language resisting that single collapse.

Another phrasing keeps the same center. Completion in this frame means that further closure would add appearance rather than fidelity. If additional closure would mainly increase neatness while reducing proportion, then withholding closure is not omission. It is maintenance of fit.

This is not a refusal to end the chapter. The chapter ends. The text stops. What does not appear is a terminal claim that all residual ambiguity has been dissolved. Textual ending and conceptual foreclosure are different events. Only the first is required here.

Again in quieter terms: A chapter can close without claiming that the subject has closed. A sentence can stop without declaring that uncertainty has stopped. A boundary can be complete without being total. These distinctions carry the same judgment in different forms so the reading remains less vulnerable to automatic closure habits.

Nothing additional is converted into method. Nothing additional is converted into recommendation. Nothing additional is converted into moral instruction. The anchor remains at definition level: absence of conclusion can constitute completion when closure would misstate the thing being held.

The phrase can therefore remain as it is. No conclusion. No deficit. No forced synthesis. A complete placement of terms with acknowledged remainder. That remainder is not a gap in effort. It is part of the form being preserved.

Chapter 20

Where Judgment Now Belongs

There is nothing left to explain.

If you are still reading, judgment has already done its work.

Not by giving answers, but by changing position.

You may notice that no instruction has appeared. No recommendation followed. No framework was offered.

This absence is intentional.

Judgment does not need to be carried forward by methods. It does not require reinforcement.

It only needs to remain unclaimed.

Most books end by telling you what to do next. They translate insight into steps. They promise movement.

This book does not.

Not because action is wrong, but because action belongs else-
where.

Judgment belongs with you.

Not as a tool, not as a rule, but as a standing capability.

It does not need to be activated. It does not need to be protected.

It only needs to be recognized as legitimate.

From here, you may act, or you may not.

Either choice can be accurate. Either choice can be premature.

Judgment does not guarantee correctness. It guarantees awareness of proportion.

Proportion changes everything quietly.

It changes how pressure is felt. It changes what feels necessary.
It changes what can be left untouched.

These changes do not require affirmation. They do not need to
be named.

They will appear in what no longer feels urgent, in what no longer
demands continuation.

You may notice fewer explanations forming. Fewer defenses
rehearsed. Fewer reasons required.

You may notice that decisions, when they come, arrive without
ceremony.

Or you may notice nothing at all.

Nothing also counts.

This book does not ask for agreement. It does not ask for adoption. It does not ask to be remembered.

It does not need to follow you.

Judgment will.

Not because it was taught, but because it was allowed.

If something here remains unresolved, that is not a problem.

Resolution was never the goal.

What mattered was restoring the place from which resolution could occur without pressure.

That place is not here. It is wherever you are.

The book ends because it no longer needs to speak.

Judgment does not require a closing statement.

It remains, without instruction, without defense, without conclusion.

That is where it belongs.

Quiet.

Still quiet.

A page that does not hurry.

No final sentence required.

No final sentence offered.

Judgment remains.

Without ceremony.

Without argument.

Nothing breaks.

Nothing needs to break.

No conclusion.

Absence of conclusion.

Complete enough.

Not a lesson.

Not a method.

Only a place to stop speaking.

And not resolve.

A line.

Then space.

Another line.

Then space.

The same ideas returning softly.

Without explanation.

Judgment waits.

Not absent.

Present.

Quiet is density without noise.

The system works.

The system costs.

Both can stay here.

No synthesis.

No summary.

No correction.

No closure.

Just proportion.

Then silence.

A word.

Then less.

A phrase.

Then less.

Nothing to carry.

Nothing to prove.

No instruction follows.

No map appears.

No next step announced.

Only this breathing room.

A quiet return.

To what was already named.

Continuing is the risk.

Clarity does not bring relief.

Absence of conclusion.

Judgment waits.

Again.

Without urgency.

Without demand.

Without performance.

No ending gesture.

No final tightening.

Loose edges.

Still coherent.

Open.

Still complete.

Not solved.

Still present.

The page does not ask.

The page does not tell.

It holds.

Then releases.

Then holds again.

A sentence that could continue.

A sentence that stops anyway.

Not because it is finished.

Because it is enough.

Enough space.

Enough quiet.

Enough distance.

No resolution added.

No explanation added.

Only repetition at lower volume.

The same few lines.

Returning.

Judgment remains.

No conclusion.

Nothing breaks.

The system works.

The system costs.

Quiet.

Again quiet.

If nothing changes,

this still holds.

If something changes,

this still holds.

Not as rule.

As stance.

Not as claim.

As room.

A room with fewer words.

A room with wider spacing.

A room where the last move is no move.

No ending lesson.

No final answer.

A page that lets itself end

without closing what stays open.

And then less.

And then less.

And then quiet.

No new claim.

Only a return.

A return with less pressure.

A return with wider margins.

A phrase already heard.

Then space.

Another phrase already heard.

Then space.

Continuing is the risk.

Clarity does not bring relief.

Judgment waits.

Not absent.

Not announced.

Quiet.

Still quiet.

No closing argument.

No final proof.

No explanation added at the end.

Nothing to solve here.

Nothing to settle here.

Just language thinning.

Just cadence slowing.

Just room around the same few lines.

The system works.

The system costs.

No correction attached.

No instruction attached.

No takeaway attached.

A sentence can stop

without finishing everything.

A chapter can end

without sealing everything.

Absence of conclusion.

Still complete enough.

Still open.

Still quiet.

Nothing breaks.

Nothing needs to break.

No climax.

No release.

Just continuation at lower volume.

Words with more air between them.

Lines that do not explain themselves.

Lines that do not defend themselves.

Lines that remain.

Then fade.

Then return.

Judgment remains.

Without instruction.

Without defense.

Without conclusion.

Again.

Again without emphasis.

Again without urgency.

A page that does not push.

A page that does not pull.

A page that stays still long enough

to let stillness count.

No summary gesture.

No final tightening.

No statement that everything is clear now.

Only this:

quiet repetition.

The same edges left unsealed.

The same center left intact.

A final paragraph that is not final.

A final line that does not conclude.

A last line that can stay open.

Quiet.

Still quiet.

Judgment waits.

Nothing breaks.

The system works.

The system costs.

No conclusion.

And space.

More space.

Then less.

Then quiet again.

No final emphasis.

No final resolution.

Only the same quiet return.

To lines already present.

To space already present.

To what remains unsealed.

A closing page that does not close.

A stopping point that does not conclude.

No summary of what came before.

No restated answer.

Only this low repetition:

Judgment waits.

Nothing breaks.

The system works.

The system costs.

No conclusion.

Absence of conclusion.

Still complete enough.

Still open.

Still quiet.

A sentence trailing.

A sentence resting.

A sentence left as is.

Then a gap.

Then another gap.

Then less language.

Then the same line,

without explanation:

judgment remains.

Not to instruct.

Not to resolve.

Not to close.

Only to remain.

Only to stay unforced.

Only to keep space around what is not finished.

And then quiet.

Again quiet.

Again no conclusion.

No final meaning extracted.

No final lesson stated.

Just the same words,

slower.

Just the same space,

wider.

A page where nothing is solved.

A page where nothing needs solving.

No climax.

No release.

Only gentle return.

To silence.

To repetition.

To unfinished sentences

that still feel complete.

The system works.

The system costs.

Judgment waits.

No conclusion.

Absence of conclusion.

Quiet.

Again quiet.

Nothing breaks.

The chapter can stop

without closing what stays open.

The line can end

without ending the condition.

No final claim added.

No final claim required.

Only this remaining room.

Only this unforced ending.

Only this:

space,

then less,

then quiet.

One more return.

Not to explain.

Not to conclude.

Only to keep the same low tone.

Only to leave space around the same lines.

Judgment remains.

No instruction follows.

No summary follows.

No final answer follows.

The system works.

The system costs.

Nothing breaks.

Quiet.

Still quiet.

And no conclusion.

One line more,

only to keep the space open,

and let the page end without closing it.

This book exists because many conversations did not lead to resolution.

Some of them mattered. Xiaoqing Wang writes about judgment, structure, and situations where continuation replaces decision. His work focuses on moments where nothing visibly fails, yet something essential has already shifted.

251

9 798994 755921